Oracle Certification Prep

Study Guide for

1Z0-034: Upgrade Oracle9i/10g OCA to Oracle Database 11g OCP

Matthew Morris

Study Guide for Upgrade Oracle9i/10g OCA to Oracle Database 11g OCP (Exam 1Z0-034) Rev 1.1

ISBN-13: 978-1-941404-06-5
ISBN-10: 1941404065

Table of Contents

What to expect from the test

The test consists of 98 multiple choice or multiple answer questions and you will have 120 minutes to complete it. This works out to about 1.3 minutes per question which means you are likely to feel a time crunch. The passing score listed on Oracle Education at this time is 61%, but as with all Oracle certification tests, they note it is subject to change.

This test is broken into two broad sections: Backup & Recovery and Database Administration. Unlike some of Oracle's exams where the sections are scored separately, 1Z0-034 has only a single score for the whole exam. Answer every question – an unanswered question counts off the same amount as an incorrect one. I have found that marking questions I'm not sure of and re-reading them again at the end of the test is valuable as sometimes later questions provide information that will answer earlier ones.

Oracle University created this test by pulling topics from several existing exams. The single largest source is 1Z0-053, but there are sections from 1Z0-052, 1Z0-050, and 1Z0-043. These are essentially the exams that 9i and 10g OCAs are skipping in order to become an 11g Oracle Certified Professional. The exam has **112 topics**. This is a huge amount of information that exam candidates must prepare for. The subjects on the exam are all over the map, but the largest single focus (66 topics) is on issues related to backup and recovery. Of those, thirty-one directly reference RMAN. If you are not familiar with using RMAN, you are extremely unlikely to pass If you were going to pick just one book to read other than this guide (and I highly suggest you do more than that), it would be Oracle's RMAN User Guide.

The 1Z0-034 exam is a convenient way for Oracle professionals with OCAs in 9i or 10g to upgrade their credentials. However, I caution you to avoid thinking that it will be an easy way to upgrade your certification. This exam is likely to be a bear and you should allocate plenty of time and effort preparing for it.

What to Expect from this Study Guide

This book is built around the subject matter topics that Oracle Education has indicated will be tested. I've gathered together material from several Oracle documentation sources along with examples to familiarize you with the types of questions you're likely to see on the exam. The guide covers a significant percentage of the information and operations that you must be familiar with in order to pass.

Candidates taking the exam should have already passed the exams to become a 9i or 10g OCA. You should have a reasonable level of knowledge of the Oracle database. If you have been working with Oracle since earning your OCA, much of the information in this guide should be familiar. If you earned your OCA years ago, but have not been working with Oracle since then, most likely you have a lot of re-learning to do.

No book in and of itself is a substitute for hands-on experience. In preparing for this exam, you should install and configure an Oracle 11g database, create users and tables, and use RMAN to create backups and perform restore operations. Practicing the concepts discussed in this guide on a test database <u>prior</u> to scheduling the exam will greatly improve your chances of passing. Since Oracle has made the Oracle XE 11g version of its database free to download and use, there is no reason why anyone who wants to learn to use Oracle 11g cannot get hands-on experience.

The goal of this guide is to present to you the concepts and information most likely to be the subject of test questions in a compact format that will allow you to read through it more than once to reinforce the information. If much of the information presented here is new to you, then you <u>need</u> to supplement this guide with other study materials. If you have a reasonable grounding in Oracle administration tasks, the guide will serve to reinforce those portions that you will likely see on the exam. If you have no experience with Oracle at all, the compressed format of this guide is not likely to be the best method for learning. It might provide you with sufficient information to pass the test, but you're likely to have serious deficiencies as an Oracle database administrator.

Additional Study Resources

The companion website to this series is www.oraclecertificationprep.com. The site contains many additional resources that can be used to study for this exam (and others). From the entry page of the website, click on the 'Exams' button, and then select the link for this test. The Exam Details page contains links to the following information sources:

- Applicable Oracle documentation.
- Third-party books relevant to the exam.
- White papers and articles on Oracle Learning Library on topics covered in the exam.
- Articles on the Web that may be useful for the exam.

The website will never link to unauthorized content such as brain dumps or illegal content such as copyrighted material made available without the consent of the author. I cannot guarantee the accuracy of the content links. While I have located the data and scanned it to ensure that it is relevant to the given exam, I did not write it and have not proofread it from a technical standpoint. The material on the Oracle Learning Library is almost certain to be completely accurate and most of the other links come from highly popular Oracle support websites and are created by experienced Oracle professionals.

I recommend that you use more than one source of study materials whenever you are preparing for a certification. Reading information presented from multiple different viewpoints can help to give you a more complete picture of any given topic. The links on the website can help you to do this. Fully understanding the information covered in this certification is not just valuable so that getting a passing score is more likely – it will also help you in your career. I guarantee that in the long run, any knowledge you gain while studying for this certification will provide more benefit to you than any piece of paper or line on your resume.

Practice Questions

The guides in the Oracle Certification Prep series do not contain example questions. The format that they are designed around is not really compatible. The concise format used for the study guides means that adding a reasonable number of questions would nearly double the size of the guides themselves. However, because practice questions have been a common request from readers of my books, I have created a series of practice tests for the exams. The practice tests are available from the companion website listed in the previous section of this guide. They are not free, but the price is a fraction of that charged by other vendors for Oracle certification practice tests.

Unlike much of the material advertised online, these tests are not brain dumps. All of the tests are original content that I developed. Using these exams will not endanger your certification status with the Oracle certification program. I submit each test to the certification team after I finish developing it so that they can verify that they do not contain illicit material. These tests serve as an inexpensive means for any certification candidate that wants to determine how successful their preparation has been before scheduling the real exam.

As a purchaser of this study guide, you can use the following promotional code to get $2.00 off the purchase price of the practice exam for 1Z0-034: **034_YBSYI.**

The tests are available at the following URL:

http://oraclecertificationprep.com/apex/f?p=OCPSG:Practice_Tests

Backup and Recovery

Backup and Recovery Concepts

Identify the types of failure that can occur in an Oracle database

There are a number of different problems that can affect the normal operation of an Oracle database or impair database I/O operations. However, the failures that require DBA intervention and data repair generally fall into one of three categories: user errors, application errors, and media failures.

- **User Errors** – These occur when data in your database is changed or deleted incorrectly through the actions of users. The root cause might be an error in application logic or a manual mistake. An example would be when a user drops a database table by mistake.
- **Application Errors** – It is possible for a software malfunction to corrupt data blocks. If this takes the form of a physical corruption (also known as a media corruption), the database does not recognize the block.
- **Media Failures** – In a media failure, a problem external to the database prevents it from reading from or writing to a database file while the instance is running. Common media failures include disk failures and the deletion of database files.

There are other failure classes. However, these do not typically result in the need for DBA intervention or media recovery:

- **Statement Failure** – If a SQL statement fails, all changes made by it will be automatically rolled back. The failure of a single SQL statement will not impact other statements in the transaction.
- **User Process Failure** – If a user session or process fails, PMON will automatically detect this and clean up after it. Any transactions that were active at the time of the failure will be rolled back and all locks held will be released.

- **Instance Failure** – If the database instance fails or is shut down with the ABORT clause, the database will perform instance recovery on the next startup.

Describe ways to tune instance recovery

Instance and crash recovery is the automatic application of redo log records to data blocks after a crash or system failure. Any time an instance is shut down cleanly, changes that are in memory but have not been written to the data files are written to disk during the shutdown checkpoint. However, if a database is shutdown with the abort option, or a single instance database crashes or if all instances of an Oracle RAC configuration crash, then this checkpoint does not occur. In these cases, the Oracle Database will perform a crash recovery on the next startup. There are two steps to instance and crash recovery: cache recovery followed by transaction recovery. Because the database can be opened once cache recovery completes, improving the performance of this step increases availability of the database.

- **Cache Recovery** – In the cache recovery step (also known as rolling forward), the Database applies all committed and uncommitted changes in the redo log files to the affected data blocks. The amount of work required for cache recovery is proportional to the rate of change for the database and the time between checkpoints.
- **Transaction Recovery** – Once all changes from the redo log are applied to the data files, any changes that were not committed at the time of the crash must be rolled back. In the transaction recovery step, the database uses rollback information to back out the uncommitted changes.

Periodically, Oracle Database records the highest system change number (SCN) for which all data blocks less than or equal to that SCN are known to be written out to the data files. This is called a checkpoint. If there is an instance failure, only redo records with changes above the last checkpoint SCN must be applied during recovery. The duration of cache recovery processing is determined by two factors: the number of data blocks that have changes at SCNs higher than the SCN of the checkpoint, and the number of log blocks that need to be read to find those changes. A database that checkpoints frequently will write dirty buffers to the data files more often. This will reduce cache recovery time in the event of an instance failure because fewer redo blocks will have to be applied to the datafiles. However, frequent checkpointing in a high-update system can reduce database performance.

Oracle's Fast-Start Fault Recovery feature is intended to reduce cache recovery time and make it more predictable. It does this by limiting the number of dirty buffers and the number of redo records generated between the most recent redo record and the last checkpoint. This feature uses the Fast-Start checkpointing architecture instead of conventional event-driven checkpointing. Instead of the bulk writes used by conventional checkpointing, fast-start checkpointing occurs incrementally. Each DBWn process periodically writes buffers to disk to advance the checkpoint position. This eliminates the I/O spikes that occur with conventional checkpointing. The FAST_START_MTTR_TARGET initialization parameter enables Fast-Start Fault Recovery and simplifies the configuration of recovery time from instance or system failure. The parameter sets a target for the expected mean time to recover (MTTR). The value of parameter is the time (in seconds) that it should take to start up the instance and perform cache recovery. Once set, the database manages incremental checkpoints in an attempt to meet that target.

Identify the importance of checkpoints, redo log files, and archived log files

Redo Logs

The redo log is the single most crucial structure for recovery operations. A redo log consists of two or more pre-allocated files that store all changes made to the database as they occur. Every Oracle database instance has an associated redo log for protection in case of an instance failure. The log files contain redo records. A redo record is a group of change vectors, each of which is a description of a change made to a single block in the database. A change made to a given table in the database will generate a redo record with change vectors for the data segment block for the table, the undo segment data block, and the transaction table of the undo segments. The information in redo entries can be used to reconstruct all changes made to the database, including the undo segments. Redo records can be written to a redo log file before the corresponding transaction has been committed. If the redo log buffer fills, or another database transaction is committed, LGWR flushes all of the entries in the redo log buffer to a redo log file. If necessary, the database can roll back any uncommitted changes. Committed changes will be written to the redo log before those changes are written to the data files. In the event of an instance failure, the redo logs are what ensure that committed database transactions are never lost.

Checkpoints

Periodically, all modified database buffers in the system global area are written to the datafiles by DBWn. This is known as a checkpoint. The checkpoint process is responsible for signaling DBWn at checkpoints and updating all the datafiles and control files of the database to indicate the most recent checkpoint. In the event of an instance failure, Oracle must know where to start when applying redo information to the datafiles. The SCN of the most recent checkpoint provides that starting point.

Archive Logs

An archived redo log file is a copy of one of the filled members of a redo log group. It includes the redo entries and the unique log sequence number of the identical member of the redo log group. Whereas redo logs are used for instance recovery, archive logs are used for media recovery. Instance recovery happens after a database crash or shutdown abort. The database files that were in use at the time of the crash are updated and made consistent using redo logs. Media recovery occurs when one or more backup copies of database data files are used for recovery. In this case, the old files must have all changes applied to them from the time the backup was taken until the present date in order to be made current. This is media recovery and requires the use of archived redo logs.

Configure ARCHIVELOG mode

In order to toggle the archiving mode of the database, use the ALTER DATABASE statement with the ARCHIVELOG or NOARCHIVELOG clause. You must be logged in to the database with administrator privileges in order to alter the archiving mode. The following steps will enable ARCHIVELOG on a database:

1. Shut down the database instance. The database must be closed and all associated instances shut down in order to switch the database archiving mode. It is also not possible to change the mode from ARCHIVELOG to NOARCHIVELOG if any datafiles need media recovery.
2. Edit the initialization parameter file. Add required parameters to specify the destinations for the archived redo log files.
3. Perform a STARTUP MOUNT on the database.
4. Change the database archiving mode by issuing ALTER DATABASE ARCHIVELOG.
5. Open the database for normal operations by issuing ALTER DATABASE OPEN.
6. Shut down the database.

7. Back up the database. Because changing the archiving mode updates the control file, you must back up all of your database files and control file. Previous backups are no longer usable.

Perform backup and recovery in NOARCHIVELOG mode

When a database is run in NOARCHIVELOG mode, archiving of the redo logs is disabled. The database control file indicates that filled groups are not required to be archived. When a filled group becomes inactive after a log switch, the group is immediately available for reuse by the LGWR process. A database running in NOARCHIVELOG mode is protected from instance failure but not from media failure. Only the changes made to the database stored in the online redo log groups are available for instance recovery. If a media failure occurs to a database that is in NOARCHIVELOG mode, it is only possible to restore the database to the point of the most recent full database backup.

A full database backup can be either consistent or inconsistent. When a backup is consistent, all read/write data files and control files have the same checkpoint SCN. This ensures that these files contain all changes up to this SCN. A consistent backup does not require recovery after it is restored and one can only be created after a consistent shutdown of the database. A database operating in NOARCHIVELOG mode can only create a valid backup of a consistent database.

If the database has been shut down with the NORMAL, IMMEDIATE, or TRANSACTIONAL options, then it is in a consistent state and you can create a usable backup by copying all of the data files with operating system commands. If the database is open, has just had an instance failure or been SHUTDOWN with the ABORT option, the database is in an inconsistent state. Copying the files at this time will create a backup that is inconsistent with the database SCN. Backups taken for a database in NOARCHIVELOG mode must be consistent. When a database is in ARCHIVELOG mode, it is possible to take inconsistent backups because the archived logs can be used to apply recovery to the datafiles to bring them to a consistent state.

Creating a user-managed consistent whole database backup:

1. Shut down the database with the NORMAL, IMMEDIATE, or TRANSACTIONAL options.

```
SQL> SHUTDOWN IMMEDIATE
SQL> STARTUP FORCE DBA
SQL> SHUTDOWN IMMEDIATE
```

2. Use an operating system utility to make backups of all data files, all control files, and the initialization parameter file.
3. Restart the database with the STARTUP command.

```
SQL> STARTUP
```

Creating a server-managed database backup

To make a consistent database backup using RMAN:

1. Start RMAN and connect to a target database.
2. Shut down the database consistently and then mount it. The following commands will guarantee that the database is in a consistent state for a backup:

```
RMAN> SHUTDOWN IMMEDIATE;
RMAN> STARTUP FORCE DBA;
RMAN> SHUTDOWN IMMEDIATE;
RMAN> STARTUP MOUNT;
```

3. Run the BACKUP DATABASE command. The following command will back up the database to the default backup device:

```
RMAN> BACKUP DATABASE;
```

4. Open the database and resume normal operations. The following command opens the database:

```
RMAN> ALTER DATABASE OPEN;
```

Restoring the database:

When performing a user-managed restore, the DBA is responsible for locating all of the required backup files and placing them in the correct locations. The basic steps to perform a user-managed complete database recovery are:

1. Shut down the database with the NORMAL, IMMEDIATE, or TRANSACTIONAL options.

```
SQL> SHUTDOWN IMMEDIATE
SQL> STARTUP FORCE DBA
SQL> SHUTDOWN IMMEDIATE
```

2. Use an operating system utility to make backups of all data files, all control files, and the initialization parameter file.
3. Restart the database with the STARTUP command.

```
SQL> STARTUP
```

When using RMAN, the RESTORE DATABASE and RECOVER DATABASE commands are used to recover the whole database. In order for the recovery to work, backups of all needed files must exist. The steps below assume that it is possible to restore all data files to their original locations. If the original locations are inaccessible, the SET NEWNAME command must be used to restore them to a different location.

To recover the whole database using RMAN:

1. Place the database in a mounted state. The following command terminates the database instance if it is started and mounts the database.

```
RMAN> STARTUP FORCE MOUNT;
```

2. Restore the database. The following command uses the preconfigured disk channel to restore the database.

```
RMAN> RESTORE DATABASE;
```

3. **Recover the database.**

```
RMAN> RECOVER DATABASE;
```

4. **Open the database.**

```
RMAN> ALTER DATABASE OPEN;
```

Configuring for Recoverability

Configure multiple archive log file destinations to increase availability

When the database is in archivelog mode, at least one destination for archived log files must be specified. However, it is possible to specify two or more destinations to provide greater redundancy. The destinations can be either to a local file system, a remote file system, or to an Oracle Automatic Storage Management (Oracle ASM) disk group. If multiple destinations are specified, a copy of each filled redo log file will be written out to every destination simultaneously. If there is a failure at one of the destinations, Oracle can make use of a copy from one of the alternate destinations during recovery.

There are two methods by which you can set the archive log file destination.

- **LOG_ARCHIVE_DEST and LOG_ARCHIVE_DUPLEX_DEST** -- For a single archive log destination, you can set only the LOG_ARCHIVE_DEST initialization parameters. To maintain a primary and secondary destination, you would specify the duplex location. These parameters can only be used for locations on the local host. Some examples are:

```
LOG_ARCHIVE_DEST = '/u01/arc'
LOG_ARCHIVE_DUPLEX_DEST = '/u02/arc'
```

- **LOG_ARCHIVE_DEST_n** -- If you wish to archive to three or more locations, you must use the alternate LOG_ARCHIVE_DEST_n initialization parameters. The value of n can be any integer from 1 to 31. Archive destinations 1 to 10 are available for local or remote locations. Archive destinations 11 to 31 are available for remote locations only. Some examples are:

```
LOG_ARCHIVE_DEST_1 = 'LOCATION=/u01/arc'
LOG_ARCHIVE_DEST_2 = 'LOCATION=/u02/arc'
LOG_ARCHIVE_DEST_3 = 'LOCATION=/u03/arc'
```

The LOCATION keyword for LOG_ARCHIVE_DEST_n can be used to specify a file system location on the current host, an Oracle ASM disk group, or the Fast Recovery Area. Examples of each of these are:

```
LOG_ARCHIVE_DEST_n = 'LOCATION=/u01/arc'
LOG_ARCHIVE_DEST_n = 'LOCATION=+DGROUP1'
LOG_ARCHIVE_DEST_n = 'LOCATION=USE_DB_RECOVERY_FILE_DEST'
```

Alternately, the SERVICE keyword for LOG_ARCHIVE_DEST_n can be used to specify remote archival through an Oracle Net service name. An example of which is:

```
LOG_ARCHIVE_DEST_n = 'SERVICE=remotedb'
```

Adding the MANDATORY keyword to a log archive destination specifies that archiving to the given destination must succeed before the redo log file can be made available for reuse

```
LOG_ARCHIVE_DEST_1 = 'LOCATION=/u01/arc MANDATORY'
```

Define, apply and use a retention policy

RMAN retention policies are intended to insure that you have sufficient redundancy in the number of database backups to prevent a catastrophic data loss while keeping you from storing so many that you run out of disk space. The RMAN command CONFIGURE RETENTION POLICY is used to define an automatic backup retention policy. The backup retention policy provides RMAN with the information required to decide if a given backup of datafiles or control files is obsolete. Obsolete backups are no longer needed for recovery. These files can be viewed using the REPORT OBSOLETE command or removed using the DELETE OBSOLETE command.

Even when a retention policy is in place, RMAN will never automatically delete backup files simply because they have become obsolete. The files will remain until removed via the DELETE OBSOLETE command. However, if a database has been configured with a fast recovery area, it is possible that obsolete files can be deleted to satisfy the fast recovery area disk quota rules. If additional space is needed for new files then the database will delete files in the fast recovery area that are either obsolete or have already been backed up to tape. However, the database will not violate the retention policy in order to free up space in the fast recovery area.

Obsolete recovery files should not be confused with expired files. The two have different definitions:

- **Obsolete** -- Backup files are obsolete when according to the current retention policy, they are no longer required for recovery.
- **Expired** -- Backup files are set to expired when an RMAN CROSSCHECK operation is performed and the file cannot be located.

Only control file backups and full or level 0 datafile backups are directly subject to retention policies. If datafiles are part of a backup set, RMAN cannot delete the set until all of the datafile backups within it are obsolete. For individual datafile copies or proxy copies, RMAN can delete them as soon as it is no longer needed according to the policy.

Incremental level 1 backups and archived redo logs become obsolete when no full backups exist that require them. RMAN initially determines which datafile and control file backups are obsolete. All incremental level 1 backups and archived logs that are not required to recover the remaining (non-obsolete) datafile or control file backup are tagged as obsolete. When using a retention policy, backup files should not be removed via non-RMAN utilities. If disk or tape files are removed via OS or media manager commands then this invalidates the ability of RMAN to intelligently control the retention of files.

There are two different types of retention policy. It is only possible to use one of them -- they are mutually exclusive.

- **Recovery Window** -- This is a rolling window of time starting with the present and extending backward in time for a set length. A recovery window defines a point of recoverability, which will be the earliest time from which it is possible to recover following a media failure. If the defined recovery window is two weeks, then RMAN retains full backups and required incremental backups and archived logs that will allow the database to be recovered up to 14 days in the past. A recovery window policy is implemented as follows:

```
CONFIGURE RETENTION POLICY TO RECOVERY WINDOW OF 14 DAYS;
```

- **Backup Redundancy** -- The redundancy retention policy specifies the number backups of each datafile to be retained. When there are more available than the number required, the oldest backups beyond the defined number are obsolete. The default retention policy is configured to REDUNDANCY 1. A backup redundancy of 3 is implemented as follows:

```
CONFIGURE RETENTION POLICY TO REDUNDANCY 3;
```

Configure the Fast Recovery Area

The Fast Recovery Area is a location in which the database can store and manage files related to backup and recovery. The location is separate from the database area, where the current database files are located. The fast recovery area can contain control files, online redo logs, archived redo logs, flashback logs, and RMAN backups. A fast recovery area minimizes the need to manually manage disk space for backup related files and balance the use of space among the different types of files. Files in the recovery area are labeled as permanent or transient.

- **Permanent files** -- These are active files used by the database instance. Permanent files that can be in the recovery area include multiplexed copies of the current control file and online redo log files.

- **Transient files** -- These files are not accessed by the database instance and are needed only during recovery operations. Transient files include: archived redo log files, foreign archived redo log files, image copies of datafiles and control files, backup pieces, and flashback logs.

Transient files are generally deleted after they become obsolete or have been backed up to tape. Files placed in the fast recovery area are maintained by Oracle Database and the generated file names use the Oracle Managed Files (OMF) format. When files are no longer needed for recovery, they become eligible for deletion when space for new files is required.

Managing Space in the Fast Recovery Area

The database issues a warning alert when reclaimable space is less than 15% and a critical alert when reclaimable space is less than 3%. An entry is added to the alert log and to the DBA_OUTSTANDING_ALERTS table to warn the DBA of this condition. If not resolved, the database will consume space in the fast recovery area until there is no space left.

You can resolve low space issues in the Fast Recovery Area in several ways:

- Make more disk space available and increase DB_RECOVERY_FILE_DEST_SIZE.
- Move backups from the fast recovery area to tertiary storage such as tape. The BACKUP RECOVERY AREA command will back up all of your recovery area files to tape.
- Run DELETE for any files that have been removed with an operating system utility. The database is not aware of file removed by OS commands.
- Run the RMAN CROSSCHECK command to have RMAN recheck the contents of the fast recovery area and identify expired files, and then use the DELETE EXPIRED command to delete every expired backup from the RMAN repository.

- Delete any unnecessary guaranteed restore points.
- Review your backup retention policy and make it less restrictive.

Information about the Fast Recovery Area is stored in the V$RECOVERY_FILE_DEST dynamic view. In addition, the column IS_RECOVERY_DET_FILE has been added to the following views: V$CONTROLFILE, V$LOGFILE, V$ARCHIVED_LOG, V$DATAFILE_COPY, V$DATAFILE, V$BACKUP_PIECE and the RMAN tables. This column has a value of YES if a file of the corresponding kind has been created in the fast recovery area.

The following initialization parameters are used to enable the Fast Recovery Area. Only the first two are required, and the database does not require a restart after they have been set.

- **DB_RECOVERY_FILE_DEST_SIZE** -- Specifies the maximum total bytes to be used by the Fast Recovery Area. The basic (minimum) recovery area size should be the sum of all the database files, plus sufficient size for incremental backups and all archive logs that have not been copied to tape. The required size varies widely depending on the backup strategy and whether flashback retention is enabled. This initialization parameter must be specified before DB_RECOVERY_FILE_DEST is enabled.
- **DB_RECOVERY_FILE_DEST** -- Location of the Fast Recovery Area. This can be a directory, file system, or Automatic Storage Management (Oracle ASM) disk group. It cannot be a raw file system.
- **DB_FLASHBACK_RETENTION_TARGET** -- Specifies the upper limit (in minutes) on how far back in time the database may be flashed back. This parameter is required only for Flashback Database.

These parameters cannot be enabled if you have set values for the parameters LOG_ARCHIVE_DEST and LOG_ARCHIVE_DUPLEX_DEST. You must disable those parameters before setting up the Fast Recovery Area. You must instead set values for the LOG_ARCHIVE_DEST_n parameters. Oracle recommends that DB_RECOVERY_FILE_DEST be set to a different value from DB_CREATE_FILE_DEST or any of the DB_CREATE_ONLINE_LOG_DEST_n initialization parameters. A warning will be written to the alert log if DB_RECOVERY_FILE_DEST equals these parameters.

Use Fast Recovery Area

Oracle recommends that archive logs be written to the fast recovery area so that the archived logs are automatically managed by the database. Because the fast recovery area is managed by OMF, the generated file names for the archived logs are not determined by the parameter LOG_ARCHIVE_FORMAT. Whether the fast recovery area is used or not, it is always best practice to create multiple copies of archived redo logs.

The following basic options for archiving redo logs are possible, listed in descending order of what Oracle considers to be best practice:

- Enable archiving to the fast recovery area only and use disk mirroring for redundancy. If DB_RECOVERY_FILE_DEST is specified and no LOG_ARCHIVE_DEST_n is specified, then LOG_ARCHIVE_DEST_1 is implicitly set to the recovery area.
- Enable archiving to the fast recovery area and set one or more LOG_ARCHIVE_DEST_n initialization parameters to locations outside the fast recovery area. The fast recovery area can be set as an archiving destination by setting any LOG_ARCHIVE_DEST_n parameter to LOCATION=USE_DB_RECOVERY_FILE_DEST.
- Set LOG_ARCHIVE_DEST_n initialization parameters to archive only to non-fast recovery area locations.

There are several RMAN commands or implicit actions that can create files in the fast recovery area:

- **BACKUP** -- If the FORMAT clause is not specified for disk backups, then RMAN creates backup pieces and image copies in the fast recovery area, with names in Oracle Managed Files (OMF) format.
- **Control File Autobackup** -- RMAN will create control file autobackups in the fast recovery area when no other destination is configured.
- **RESTORE ARCHIVELOG** -- RMAN will restore archived redo log files to the fast recovery area unless the SET ARCHIVELOG DESTINATION is specifically set elsewhere.
- **RECOVER...** -- The RECOVER DATABASE, RECOVER TABLESPACE, and RECOVER ... BLOCK options restore archived redo log files from backup to the recovery area for use during media recovery. RMAN will automatically delete the files after they are applied.
- **FLASHBACK DATABASE** -- As with the RECOVER... options, RMAN will pull any required archived log files to the recovery area and delete them after they have been applied.

Using the RMAN Recovery Catalog

Identify situations that require RMAN recovery catalog

The RMAN recovery catalog is a database schema in an Oracle database that is used to store metadata about one or more Oracle databases. The data from this schema is used by RMAN when performing recovery operations. While the catalog can be stored in a database used for other purposes, it is generally stored in a dedicated database. The catalog stores information about RMAN operations for all of the target databases that have been registered in it. Any time that RMAN is connected to a recovery catalog, all metadata will be pulled exclusively from the catalog instead of the control file. By centralizing the metadata for all your target databases, the recovery catalog makes reporting and administration easier. A recovery catalog includes:

- Datafile and archived redo log backup sets and backup pieces
- Datafile copies
- Archived redo logs and their copies
- Database structure (tablespaces and datafiles)
- Stored scripts, which are named user-created sequences of RMAN commands
- Persistent RMAN configuration settings

Recovery files are required in the following cases:

- **Loss of control files** -- If the current control file and all backups are lost for a given database, a recovery catalog is required. Recovery catalogs contain the same metadata as the RMAN repository stored in the control file of each target database.
- **Recovery from very old backup** -- The control file contains a more limited amount of history than a recovery catalog. If you need to perform a recovery from a backup that goes back further in time than is stored in the control file, then a recovery catalog is required.

- **RMAN Scripts** -- RMAN scripts can be stored in a recovery catalog. The scripts are then available to every RMAN client that can connect to the target database and recovery catalog. By contrast, command files are only available if the RMAN client has access to the file system on which they are stored.
- **Data Guard** -- If you want to use RMAN in a Data Guard environment, a recovery catalog is required. The recovery catalog stores RMAN metadata for all primary and standby databases.

Create and configure a recovery catalog

Before creating a recovery catalog, you must determine what database to put it in and what schema to use. You should not put the catalog in a database that will itself be a target of the catalog. Using a dedicated catalog database is the normal and suggested option. In addition, the catalog database should not be on the same hard drive as any of its target databases or a single hard drive failure can take out both the target database and the catalog required to recover the target. The greater the independence between the catalog and target databases, the more robust the recovery scenario becomes. Once a database is selected, the catalog will be stored in a schema on that database (which cannot be SYS).

The space required by the catalog schema depends primarily on the number of databases that will be targets of the catalog. The size will also increase as the number of backups and archived log files for each individual database grows. RMAN scripts stored in the catalog will use space as well. The Oracle Database Backup and Recovery User's Guide contains more information and formulas on estimating size requirements.

Once a catalog database and schema have been determined and sufficient space exists in the catalog tablespace, you can create the schema owner and grant the schema all of the privileges required. In the example below, a dedicated database (catdb) with a tablespace called RMANCAT_TS exists. The SYS user has connected to catdb with SYSDBA privileges.

To create the recovery catalog schema and set up the default and temporary tablespaces:

```
SQL>  CREATE USER recodude IDENTIFIED BY [password]
      TEMPORARY TABLESPACE temp
      DEFAULT TABLESPACE rmancat_ts
      QUOTA UNLIMITED ON rmancat_ts;
```

Grant the RECOVERY_CATALOG_OWNER role to the rman schema.

```
SQL> GRANT RECOVERY_CATALOG_OWNER TO recodude;
```

Once the catalog schema exists, the RMAN CREATE CATALOG command is used to create the catalog tables in the default tablespace of the catalog owner. To create the recovery catalog you must start RMAN and connect to the catalog database as the recovery catalog owner. Once connected, run the CREATE CATALOG command to create the catalog. This can take several minutes.

```
RMAN> CREATE CATALOG;
```

You can specify the tablespace name for the catalog in the CREATE CATALOG command to store it in a tablespace other than the default for the schema:

```
RMAN> CREATE CATALOG TABLESPACE users;
```

Registering a Database

Once a catalog exists, you must register the target databases in the catalog. Until a database has been registered, RMAN cannot store any metadata about backup operations in the catalog. Unregistered databases will continue to use the control file as their sole source of RMAN metadata during backup and recovery operations. To register a new target database, you must:

Start RMAN and connect to both the target database and to the recovery catalog. The database contained the recovery catalog must be open and the target database must be mounted.

```
% rman TARGET / CATALOG recodude@catdb
```

Register the target database in the connected recovery catalog via the REGISTER DATABASE command:

```
REGISTER DATABASE;
```

RMAN will add information about the target database to the appropriate catalog tables. It then copies information from the control file of the target database into the catalog to synchronize the catalog with the control file. Once the command has completed, you can verify that the registration was successful by running the REPORT SCHEMA command:

```
REPORT SCHEMA;

Report of database schema
File Size(MB)  Tablespace       RB segs Datafile Name
---- ---------- ---------------- ------- --------------------
1        327680 SYSTEM             NO    /u01/oradata/system01.dbf
2         30720 UNDOTBS            YES   /u01/oradata/undotbs01.dbf
3         20480 INDEX_TS           NO    /u01/oradata/index_ts01.dbf
4         10240 TOOLS_TS           NO    /u01/oradata/tools_ts01.dbf
5         20480 USER_TS            NO    /u01/oradata/user_ts01.dbf
```

When you first create the recovery catalog, it is possible that you have datafile copies, backup pieces, or archived logs on disk that have aged out of the control file. It is possible to add them to the recovery catalog with the CATALOG command. Doing this allows RMAN to make use of use the older backups during restore operations. The following commands can be used to add files to the catalog:

- **CATALOG DATAFILECOPY** -- Allows you to add a data file backup to the catalog.
- **CATALOG ARCHIVELOG** -- Allows you to add one or more archived log files to the catalog.
- **CATALOG BACKUPPIECE** -- Allows you to add a backup piece to the catalog.
- **CATALOG START WITH** -- Allows you to add multiple files from a given directory to the catalog. RMAN will list the files to be added to the RMAN repository and prompts for confirmation before adding the backups.

When using the CATALOG START WITH command, you should be aware that if multiple directory paths contain the text supplied, you may catalog files that you did not intend to. Consider a file system that has one directory called **/u01/backups** and another called **/u01/backups/old** that contain backup files. Issuing the following command catalogs all files in both directories:

```
CATALOG START WITH '/u01/backups';
```

To catalog only backups in the /u01/backups directory, the correct command should be:

```
CATALOG START WITH '/u01/backups/';
```

Synchronize the recovery catalog

Synchronizing the recovery catalog is the process of comparing the recovery catalog to the control file (either the current or the backup) and updating the catalog with any metadata that has been changed or is not present on the catalog. RMAN automatically resynchronizes the catalog when most commands are issued, so long as the target control file is mounted and the catalog is available. It is possible to perform a full or a partial resynchronization of the catalog.

- **Partial** -- During a partial resynchronization, RMAN will update changed metadata about new backups, new archived redo logs, and so on from the target control file. Metadata in the catalog about the database physical schema will not be updated.
- **Full** -- In a full resynchronization, RMAN will locate and update all changed metadata records, including those for the database schema. A full resynchronization is performed only after structural changes have been made to the database (such as changes to database files) or if the RMAN persistent configuration has been altered.

During a full resynchronization, RMAN will create a temporary backup called a snapshot control file. This file is used to ensure that RMAN has a consistent view of the control file. It is intended only to be used for a short period of time and is not registered in the catalog. The control file checkpoint is maintained in the recovery catalog to verify the catalog currency.

If RMAN is connected to the target database and the recovery catalog, it will automatically resynchronize the recovery catalog whenever commands are executed. You should seldom need to manually resynchronize the catalog. However, there are times when it is required:

- **Catalog Unavailability** -- If you issue RMAN commands at a time when the recovery catalog is unavailable, you should open the catalog database later and use the RESYNC CATALOG command to resynchronize it manually. This might be the case if your target database and catalog database are in different locations and the availability of both at the same time cannot be guaranteed.
- **Infrequent Backups** -- If a target database running in ARCHIVELOG mode is backed up infrequently, it possible that a significant number of redo logs are archived between database backups. The recovery catalog is not updated automatically when a redo log switch occurs or when a redo log is archived. Metadata about redo log switches and archived redo logs is stored only in the control file. When RMAN backup operations are infrequent, you should regularly issue a RESYNC CATALOG to ensure this information is stored in the recovery catalog.

- **Standby Database** -- It is possible to create or alter the RMAN configuration for a standby database while not connected to the database as TARGET. After doing so, to update the control file of the standby database you can resynchronize the standby database manually.
- **Prevent Loss of Metadata** -- The data in the recovery catalog originates from the control file and the data in the control file is only kept for a limited time before being overwritten. You must ensure that the catalog is synchronized with the control file before uncataloged metadata gets overwritten. The initialization parameter CONTROL_FILE_RECORD_KEEP_TIME sets the minimum number of days that records are guaranteed to be kept in the control file. The catalog must be resynchronized at intervals less than that value by either performing backup operations that implicitly resynchronize the catalog or performing manual resynchronizations.

The RESYNC CATALOG command forces a full resynchronization of the recovery catalog. The steps to perform this are:

- Start RMAN and connect to a target database and recovery catalog.
- Mount or open the target database if it is not already mounted or open via the STARTUP MOUNT command.
- Resynchronize the recovery catalog using the RESYNC CATALOG command at the RMAN prompt.

Create and use RMAN stored scripts

RMAN recovery catalogs allow for the creation of stored scripts. Stored scripts act much like RMAN command files. However, command files require access to the file system where they are saved, whereas stored scripts require only a connection to the catalog. The CREATE SCRIPT command is used to create a stored script in the recovery catalog. It allows you to create a named sequence of RMAN commands in the recovery catalog for later execution. The CREATE SCRIPT command can only be executed from the RMAN prompt while connected to a target database and an open recovery catalog. Stored scripts can be either Global or Local:

- **GLOBAL** -- A global script is available for use with any database registered in the recovery catalog. Global scripts are available to virtual private catalogs with read-only access. It is only possible to create or update global scripts while connected to the base recovery catalog.
- **LOCAL** -- Local scripts created for the current target database only. They are not available to virtual private catalogs.

Local and Global scripts have different namespaces. It is possible to have a local and a global script of the same name. It is not possible to have two global scripts of the same name or two local scripts of the same name for a given target database.

Stored scripts can make use of substitution variables. &1 indicates where to place the first value, &2 indicate where to place the second value, and so on. If any special characters are included, they must be quoted. The syntax for substitution variables is &integer followed by an optional period. When the substitution variable is parsed, the optional period is replaced with the value. This allows the substitution text to be followed by another integer. In the following three cases, the value **orcl_backup** is passed:

- &1 -> orcl_backup
- &1.1 -> orcl_backup1
- &1..1 -> orcl_backup.1

Stored scripts with substitution variables must be provided with example values at create time. These values can be provided explicitly with the USING clause when starting RMAN or they can be entered when prompted.

Create a Local Stored Script

After starting RMAN, connect to the target database as TARGET, and connect to a recovery catalog. The following steps create a stored script called full_backup and then run it:

```
RMAN> CONNECT TARGET SYS@oraprod

target database Password: [password]
connected to target database: PROD (DBID=38752058)

RMAN> CONNECT CATALOG recodude@catdb

recovery catalog database Password: [password]
connected to recovery catalog database

RMAN> CREATE SCRIPT full_backup
COMMENT "Perform full backup of database and archive logs"
{
    BACKUP
      INCREMENTAL LEVEL 0 TAG full_backup
      FORMAT "/u02/backup/%U"
      DATABASE PLUS ARCHIVELOG;
}

RMAN> RUN { EXECUTE SCRIPT full_backup; }
```

Create a Global Stored Script

This example creates a global script that backs up the database and archived redo log files:

```
RMAN> CONNECT TARGET SYS@oraprod

target database Password: [password]
connected to target database: ORAPROD (DBID=38752058)

RMAN> CONNECT CATALOG recoman@catdb

recovery catalog database Password: [password]
connected to recovery catalog database

RMAN> CREATE GLOBAL SCRIPT global_full_backup
     { BACKUP DATABASE PLUS ARCHIVELOG; }
```

This script can now be accessed while connected to a different database:

```
RMAN> CONNECT TARGET SYS@oradev

target database Password: [password]
connected to target database: ORADEV (DBID=39823641)

RMAN> CONNECT CATALOG recoman@catdb

recovery catalog database Password: [password]
connected to recovery catalog database

RMAN> RUN { EXECUTE SCRIPT global_full_backup; }
```

Create a Stored Script with Substitution Variables

The following example connects creates a backup script that includes three substitution variables. As the last step in creating the script, RMAN prompts for initial values for the substitution variables.

```
RMAN> CONNECT TARGET /
RMAN> CONNECT CATALOG recoman@catdb

recovery catalog database Password: [password]
connected to recovery catalog database

RMAN> CREATE SCRIPT datafile_backup
2> { BACKUP DATAFILE &1 TAG &2 FORMAT '/u01/&3_%U'; }
Enter value for 1: 1

Enter value for 2: dfile1_bkup

Enter value for 3: dfile1

created script datafile_backup
```

When the script is executed, it is possible to pass different values to it:

```
RMAN> RUN { EXECUTE SCRIPT backup_df USING 2 dfile2_bkup dfile2; }
```

After the values are substituted, the script executes as follows:

```
BACKUP DATAFILE 2 TAG dfile2_bkup FORMAT '/u01/dfile2_%U';
```

Deleting a stored script

You can delete stored scripts with the DELETE SCRIPT command. The following example deletes the global script named global_full_backup:

```
RMAN> DELETE GLOBAL SCRIPT global_full_backup;

deleted global script: global_full_backup
```

Replacing an Existing Script

You can overwrite an existing stored script using the REPLACE SCRIPT command. The following example shows how to replace an existing script:

```
RMAN> CONNECT TARGET SYS@oraprod

target database Password: [password]
connected to target database: ORAPROD (DBID=38752058)

RMAN> CONNECT CATALOG recoman@catdb

recovery catalog database Password: [password]
connected to recovery catalog database

RMAN> CREATE SCRIPT full_backup
COMMENT "Perform full backup of database and archive logs"
{
    BACKUP
      INCREMENTAL LEVEL 0 TAG full_backup
      FORMAT "/u02/backup/%U"
      DATABASE;
}
```

The LIST SCRIPT NAMES command will list all scripts known to the recovery catalog:

```
RMAN> LIST SCRIPT NAMES;

List of Stored Scripts in Recovery Catalog


    Scripts of Target Database ORAPROD


       Script Name
       Description
       -------------------------------------------------
       full_backup
       Perform full backup of database and archive logs

       datafile_backup
```

However -- the script description is incorrect. As created, it does not back up the archive logs. You can replace the script with the following command:

```
RMAN> REPLACE SCRIPT full_backup
COMMENT "Perform full backup of database and archive logs"
{
    BACKUP
      INCREMENTAL LEVEL 0 TAG full_backup
      FORMAT "/u02/backup/%U"
      DATABASE PLUS ARCHIVELOG;
}
replaced script full_backup
```

Note that if you are replacing a Global script, you must use the REPLACE GLOBAL SCRIPT command.

Viewing stored scripts

The PRINT SCRIPT command allows you to see what actions are performed by a stored script:

```
RMAN> PRINT SCRIPT full_backup;

printing stored script: full_backup
 { BACKUP
      INCREMENTAL LEVEL 0 TAG full_backup
      FORMAT "/u02/backup/%U"
      DATABASE PLUS ARCHIVELOG;
 }
```

Back up the recovery catalog

When creating a backup strategy, you must be sure that it includes backing up the recovery catalog database. If a hardware failure destroys the database holding your recovery catalog, this will lose the metadata for all of your target databases. Losing the metadata will make any recovery of those databases considerably more difficult. The recovery catalog database should be backed up as often as the target databases. As a general rule, the recovery catalog should be backed up on the same schedule as your target databases and after the last has completed. For example, if you have three databases being backed up each week, one each Thursday, Friday, and Saturday, then back up the recovery catalog database on Sunday. Having a backup of the recovery catalog will be useful in a disaster recovery scenario. In a situation where you have to restore the recovery catalog database, the record of backups in the restored recovery catalog database will allow you to restore any of the three target databases.

RMAN can be used to make the backups for the recovery catalog database. However, since you will be backing up the catalog itself, start RMAN with the NOCATALOG option so that RMAN will use the control file of the catalog database for the metadata repository. The following guidelines should be used for a recovery catalog backup strategy:

- The recovery catalog database should always be run in ARCHIVELOG mode.
- The retention policy should be set to a REDUNDANCY value greater than 1.

- Use two separate media to back up the database (i.e. disk and tape).
- Execute BACKUP DATABASE PLUS ARCHIVELOG at regular intervals.
- Use the control file rather than another recovery catalog as the metadata repository.
- Configure the control file autobackup feature to ON.

Create and use a virtual private catalog

A virtual private catalog is a set of synonyms and views that enable user access to a subset of the base recovery catalog. Prior to Oracle 11g, access to the RMAN recovery catalog was an all-or-nothing proposition. Now it's possible to grant catalog access for a specific subset of databases to a given user. The owner of the base recovery catalog can GRANT or REVOKE restricted access to the catalog. Each VPC user has full read/write access to the metadata in the virtual private catalog granted to them. The RMAN metadata is stored in the schema of the virtual private catalog owner. Virtual catalog users cannot modify global RMAN scripts, although they can execute them.

Creating a virtual private catalog for a database user involves four steps from three locations. The first two steps are from the SQL*Plus as a user with admin privileges. The third step is executed from RMAN as the base catalog owner. The fourth step is executed from RMAN as the virtual private catalog user. The four steps are:

1. Create the VPC User.
2. Grant recovery_catalog_owner to the VPC user.
3. Grant the catalog to the new VPC user.
4. Create the virtual catalog.

From SQL*Plus, connected to the base recovery catalog database with administrator privileges:

```
SQL> CREATE USER vpc1 IDENTIFIED BY password
2 DEFAULT TABLESPACE vpcusers
3 QUOTA UNLIMITED ON vpcusers;
SQL> GRANT recovery_catalog_owner TO vpc1;
SQL> EXIT
```

From RMAN, connected to the recovery catalog database as the catalog owner catowner:

```
RMAN> CONNECT CATALOG catowner@catdb
recovery catalog database Password: password
connected to recovery catalog database
RMAN> GRANT CATALOG FOR DATABASE prod1 TO vpc1;
RMAN> EXIT;
```

From RMAN connected to the recovery catalog database as the virtual private catalog owner:

```
RMAN> CONNECT CATALOG vpc1@catdb
recovery catalog database Password: password
connected to recovery catalog database
RMAN> CREATE VIRTUAL CATALOG;
RMAN> EXIT;
```

Configuring Backup Specifications

Configure backup settings

RMAN has a number of different settings to control the specific actions taken during backups. The default settings for most of these parameters make sense for performing standard backup and recovery operations. Understanding what these parameters are will allow you to optimize the behavior for a given database. Persistent settings can be set for each target database, such as backup destinations, device type, and retention policy. The two commands of interest for this purpose are:

- **SHOW** -- This command displays the current value of settings configured for RMAN in the target database. The command will indicate whether or not the current values are set to their default. This information is also available in the V$RMAN_CONFIGURATION view.
- **CONFIGURE** -- This command allows you to change RMAN current behavior for your backup and recovery environment. If used with the keyword CLEAR, this command will reset the parameter to the default RMAN value. Some examples of the options that can be set follow:

Set the backup retention policy

The following command sets the backup retention policy to maintain three full or level 0 backups of each data file and control file. Any backups older than the third file are considered obsolete. The default value is 1.

```
CONFIGURE RETENTION POLICY TO REDUNDANCY 3;
```

Alternately, the retention policy can be given a recovery window that ensures sufficient backups are kept to recover the database to any point in time back to the supplied value:

```
CONFIGURE RETENTION POLICY TO RECOVERY WINDOW OF 7 DAYS;
```

Set the default device type

When a destination device type is not specific for a backup, RMAN sends it to whatever device type is configured as the default. RMAN is preset to use disk as the default device type. The following command allows you to change the default device type to tape:

```
CONFIGURE DEFAULT DEVICE TYPE TO sbt;
```

Regardless of the default device type, you can specifically direct a backup to a specific device type using the DEVICE TYPE clause of the BACKUP command, as shown in the following examples:

```
BACKUP DEVICE TYPE SBT DATABASE;
BACKUP DEVICE TYPE DISK DATABASE;
```

Set the default backup type

When backing up to disk, RMAN can be configured to create either backup sets or image copies by default (the backup type for tape can only be a backup set). In addition, RMAN can create backup sets using binary compression. Specifying the COMPRESSED option in the BACKUP TYPE TO ... BACKUPSET clause configures RMAN to use compressed backup sets by default for a given device type. Omitting the COMPRESSED keyword, disables compression. The preconfigured backup type for disk is an uncompressed backup set. The following examples show configuring RMAN backups to copies and backup sets:

```
CONFIGURE DEVICE TYPE DISK BACKUP TYPE TO BACKUPSET;
CONFIGURE DEVICE TYPE DISK BACKUP TYPE TO COPY;
```

To enable compression on backupsets, you would add the COMPRESSED keyword:

```
CONFIGURE DEVICE TYPE DISK BACKUP TYPE TO COMPRESSED BACKUPSET;
CONFIGURE DEVICE TYPE SBT BACKUP TYPE TO COMPRESSED BACKUPSET;
```

Configuring Channels

An RMAN channel is a connection to a database server session. The CONFIGURE CHANNEL command is used to configure options for disk or SBT channels. When the CONFIGURE CHANNEL command is used to specify default channel settings for a device, any previous settings are lost. Any settings not specified in the CONFIGURE CHANNEL command will be returned to their default value.

```
CONFIGURE CHANNEL DEVICE TYPE DISK MAXPIECESIZE 1G;
CONFIGURE CHANNEL DEVICE TYPE DISK FORMAT /tmp/%U;
```

Configuring Channels for Disk

RMAN allocates a single disk channel for all operations by default. You can change the default location and format for the file name for that channel. Be aware that when an explicit format is configured for disk channels, RMAN does not create backups by default in the fast recovery area.

```
CONFIGURE CHANNEL DEVICE TYPE DISK FORMAT '/u01/ora_df%t_s%s_s%p';
CONFIGURE CHANNEL DEVICE TYPE DISK FORMAT '+dgroup1';
```

Set the parallelism for a device

When multiple channels are available, RMAN can read or write in parallel. The number of channels should normally match the number of devices available (i.e. three tape drives = three channels). Allocating multiple channels for a single device can negatively affect performance unless your disk subsystem is optimized for multiple channels. The channel parallelism can be set for each device type as follows.

```
CONFIGURE DEVICE TYPE SBT PARALLELISM 2;
```

The command above only affects the parallelism for tape devices and does not alter the values of other device settings not specified.

Configure Control File and Server Parameter File Autobackups

RMAN can be set to automatically back up the control file and server parameter file whenever a backup record is added. In addition, if the database structure metadata in the control file changes and the database is in ARCHIVELOG mode, an autobackup will be taken. Control file autobackup adds additional redundancy to the recovery strategy, allowing RMAN to recover the database even after the loss of the current control file, recovery catalog, and server parameter file. The autobackup feature is enabled and disabled as follows:

```
CONFIGURE CONTROLFILE AUTOBACKUP ON;
CONFIGURE CONTROLFILE AUTOBACKUP OFF;
```

Resetting default values

The RMAN configuration settings can be returned to their default values by using the CLEAR keyword:

```
CONFIGURE DEFAULT DEVICE TYPE CLEAR;
CONFIGURE RETENTION POLICY CLEAR;
CONFIGURE CONTROLFILE AUTOBACKUP CLEAR;
```

Allocate channels to use in backing up

A channel is a connection between RMAN and a database instance. Channels specified via the CONFIGURE command will be allocated automatically. You can also allocate channels manually by using ALLOCATE CHANNEL within a RUN block. If ALLOCATE CHANNEL is not specified for a given job, then the automatic channels will be applied. It is possible to allocate up to 255 channels and each channel can read up to 64 files in parallel. When multiple channels are allocated to a job, RMAN can read or write multiple backup sets or disk copies in parallel. Each channel operates on a single backup set or image copy at a time. When the job is complete, RMAN will release the channel. The basic guidelines for channels are:

- **DISK** -- You should allocate one channel for each output device. If the backup is being written to a striped file system or an ASM disk group, allocating multiple channels can improve performance.
- **TAPE** -- The number of tape channels should equal the number of tape devices divided by the number of duplexed copies.

Manually Allocating a Channel for a Backup

This example allocates a single tape channel for a whole database and archived redo log backup. The PARMS parameter specifies the Tivoli Storage Manager media family.

```
RUN
{
  ALLOCATE CHANNEL c1 DEVICE TYPE sbt
    PARMS
'ENV=(TDPO_OPTFILE=/opt/tivoli/tsm/client/oracle/bin64/tdpo.opt)';
  BACKUP DATABASE;
  BACKUP ARCHIVELOG ALL NOT BACKED UP;
}
```

Distributing a Backup Across Multiple Disks

It is possible to spread a backup across multiple hard drives. You must allocate a channel of DEVICE TYPE DISK for each disk drive and specify the format string.

```
RUN
{
  ALLOCATE CHANNEL U01 DEVICE TYPE DISK FORMAT '/u01/%U';
  ALLOCATE CHANNEL U02 DEVICE TYPE DISK FORMAT '/u02/%U';
  BACKUP DATABASE PLUS ARCHIVELOG;
}
```

Configure backup optimization

When RMAN backup optimization is enabled, RMAN will skip files during a backup operation if the identical file has already been backed up to the currently specified device type. In order to determine of the file is truly identical, RMAN uses the following criteria:

- **Datafile** --The datafile must have the same DBID, checkpoint SCN, creation SCN, and RESETLOGS SCN and time as a datafile already in a backup. The datafile must be offline-normal, read-only, or closed normally.
- **Archived log** -- The log must have the same DBID, thread, sequence number, and RESETLOGS SCN and time
- **Backup set** -- The backup set must have the same DBID, backup set record ID, and stamp.

Even if RMAN determines that the file is identical to one that has already been backed up, the retention policy or the backup duplexing feature may require it to be backed up. Also, if the TO DESTINATION is used in conjunction with BACKUP RECOVERY AREA or BACKUP RECOVERY FILES, RMAN will only look for identical backups in the specific TO DESTINATION location provided. Backup optimization is enabled by issuing the following command:

```
CONFIGURE BACKUP OPTIMIZATION ON;
```

Once backup optimization has been configured for a target database, if none of the backed-up files specified for a given job has changed since the last backup, then RMAN will not back up the files again. Even if every file for a given backup is skipped because the files have already been backed up, no error will occur. Backup optimization can be overridden by including the FORCE keyword in the BACKUP command:

```
BACKUP DATABASE FORCE;
BACKUP ARCHIVELOG ALL FORCE;
```

Using RMAN to Create Backups

Create image file backups

When RMAN creates image copies, the result is bit-for-bit copies of each data file, archived redo log file, or control file. Images copies can be used as-is to perform recovery. They are generated with the RMAN BACKUP AS COPY command, an operating system command such as the UNIX cp, or by the Oracle archiver process. The default RMAN backup type can be set to image using the CONFIGURE DEVICE TYPE COMMAND:

```
CONFIGURE DEVICE TYPE DISK BACKUP TYPE TO COPY;
```

It is also possible to override the default with the AS COPY clause of the BACKUP command:

```
BACKUP AS COPY
  DEVICE TYPE DISK
  DATABASE;
```

The other format type is backup sets. Backup sets consist of one or more data files, control files, server parameter files, and archived redo log files. Each backup set consists of one or more binary files. Each binary file is called a backup piece. Backup pieces are written in a proprietary format that can only be created or restored by RMAN. The contents of a backup set are divided among multiple backup pieces only if the backup piece size is limited using MAXPIECESIZE. This keyword is an option of the ALLOCATE CHANNEL or CONFIGURE CHANNEL command. As with image copies, the default type is set with the CONFIGURE DEVICE TYPE command:

```
CONFIGURE DEVICE TYPE DISK BACKUP TYPE TO BACKUPSET;
```

The default can be overridden using the AS BACKUPSET clause. You can allow backup sets to be created on the configured default device, or direct them specifically to disk or tape.

```
BACKUP AS BACKUPSET
  DATABASE;

BACKUP AS BACKUPSET
  DEVICE TYPE DISK
  DATABASE;
```

Create a whole database backup

A whole database backup includes a backup of the control file and all data files that belong to a database. A whole database backup can be made with the database mounted or open. The RMAN command BACKUP DATABASE is used to perform a whole database backup.

```
BACKUP DATABASE;
```

Adding the PLUS ARCHIVELOGS clause will back up the database, switch the online redo logs, and include archived logs in the backup. This guarantees that you have the full set of archived logs through the time of the backup and guarantees that you can perform media recovery after restoring this backup.

```
BACKUP DATABASE PLUS ARCHIVELOG;
```

Enable fast incremental backup

The block change tracking feature improves backup performance for incremental backups by recording changed blocks for each data file. If block change tracking is enabled, RMAN uses a block change tracking file to identify changed blocks during incremental backups. This file keeps RMAN from having to scan every block in the data file that it is backing up. Block change tracking is disabled by default. A single block change tracking file is created for the whole database. By default, the change tracking file is created as an Oracle managed file in the destination specified by the DB_CREATE_FILE_DEST initialization parameter.

To enable block change tracking, execute the following ALTER DATABASE statement:

```
ALTER DATABASE ENABLE BLOCK CHANGE TRACKING;
```

You can also create the change tracking file in a specific location:

```
ALTER DATABASE ENABLE BLOCK CHANGE TRACKING
USING FILE '/ocpdir/rman_change_track.f' REUSE;
```

You can disable block change tracking by executing the following command:

```
ALTER DATABASE DISABLE BLOCK CHANGE TRACKING;
```

The V$BLOCK_CHANGE_TRACKING view can be used to determine whether change tracking is enabled, and the file name of the block change tracking file.

```
SELECT status, filename
FROM   v$block_change_tracking;

STATUS   FILENAME
-------- ----------------------------------------------------
ENABLED  /u01/ocp/RDBMS/changetracking/e1_cs_2e61nr6j_.chg
```

Create duplex backup and back up backup sets

RMAN has the ability to create up to four duplexed copies when creating a backup set. Duplexing is not possible when making image copies. Duplexing is enabled using the COPIES parameter in the CONFIGURE, SET, or BACKUP commands. When duplexing, RMAN produces a single backup set with a unique key, and generates the requested number of identical copies of each backup piece in the set. It is possible to duplex backups to either disk or tape, but not to tape and disk simultaneously. The FORMAT parameter of the BACKUP command sets the destinations for the backup sets. The number of copies should never exceed the number of available tape devices when backup up to tape. Duplexing backup sets to the fast recovery area is not possible. The following command creates two backup set copies of data file 3:

```
BACKUP DEVICE TYPE DISK COPIES 2 DATAFILE 3
  FORMAT '/u01/%U','/u02/%U';
```

It is also possible to use CONFIGURE BACKUP COPIES to enable duplexing by default. The default setting will apply to all backup sets except control file autobackups and backupsets that are backed up using the BACKUP BACKUPSET command. By default, CONFIGURE ... BACKUP COPIES is set to 1 for disk and tape. The following example sets duplexing for datafiles and archivelog files on disk to two.

```
CONFIGURE CHANNEL DEVICE TYPE DISK FORMAT '/u01/%U', '/u02/%U';
CONFIGURE DATAFILE BACKUP COPIES FOR DEVICE TYPE DISK TO 2;
CONFIGURE ARCHIVELOG BACKUP COPIES FOR DEVICE TYPE DISK TO 2;
```

Given the above configuration, the following command backs up the database and archived logs to disk, making two copies of each data file and archived log, placing one copy of the backup sets produced in the /u01 directory and the other in the /u02 directory:

```
BACKUP DEVICE TYPE DISK AS BACKUPSET DATABASE PLUS ARCHIVELOG;;
```

Backups of Backup Sets

You can use RMAN to make copies of existing previously created backup sets with the BACKUP BACKUPSET command. This will back up backup sets that were created on disk and can be used to spread backups among multiple media. If RMAN determines that a backup set is corrupted or missing, it will search for other copies of the same backup set. The following example backs up existing backup sets to tape to ensure that all your backups exist on both media types.

```
BACKUP DEVICE TYPE DISK AS BACKUPSET
  DATABASE PLUS ARCHIVELOG;
BACKUP
  DEVICE TYPE sbt
  BACKUPSET ALL;
```

The BACKUP BACKUPSET can also be used to manage backup space allocation. The following backs up backup sets that were created more than 14 days ago from disk to tape, and then deletes the backup sets from disk. If a backup was duplexed to multiple locations on disk, RMAN will delete all copies of the pieces in the backup set.

```
BACKUP
  DEVICE TYPE SBT
  BACKUPSET COMPLETED BEFORE 'SYSDATE-14'
  DELETE INPUT;
```

Create an archival backup for long-term retention

The RMAN KEEP option specifies that a backup be created as an archival backup. An archival backup is a self-contained backup that is exempt from the configured retention policy. Archival backups contain all of the files necessary to restore the backup and recover it to a consistent state. If the database is open at the time an archival backup is created, RMAN automatically generates and backs up the redo logs needed to make the backup consistent. When available, RMAN will use archival backups for disaster recovery restore operations. However, their intended purpose is to produce a snapshot of the database that can be restored on another system for testing or historical usage.

KEEP

When computing the retention policy RMAN does not consider backup pieces with the KEEP option. The KEEP option cannot be used to override the retention policy for files stored in the fast recovery area. When KEEP is specified, RMAN backs up datafiles, archived redo logs, the control file, and the server parameter file. A recovery catalog is required when KEEP FOREVER is specified because the backup records will eventually age out of the control file.

UNTIL TIME 'date_string'

This clause specifies an end date for retaining the RMAN backup or copy. After this date the backup is obsolete, regardless of the backup retention policy settings. It's possible to provide a specific date/time by using the current NLS_DATE_FORMAT, or a SQL date expression such as 'SYSDATE+90'. If a KEEP TIME is provided with a date only, then the backup becomes obsolete one second after midnight on that date.

RESTORE POINT restore_point_name

Creates a restore point matching the SCN to which RMAN must recover the backup to a consistent state. The name provided must not already exist. RMAN captures the SCN immediately after the datafile backups complete. The restore point acts as a label for the SCN to which this archival backup can be restored.

NOKEEP

This option indicates that any KEEP attributes no longer apply to the backup. After specifying NOKEEP, the backup is subject to the configured backup retention

Create a multisection, compressed and encrypted backup

Multisection Backups

Multisection backups enable RMAN channels to back up a single large file in parallel. The work is divided among multiple channels, with each channel backing up one file section in a file. This can improve the performance of backups of large datafiles. Multisection backups are enabled by specifying the SECTION SIZE parameter on the BACKUP command. Each file section is a contiguous range of blocks in a file. The SECTION SIZE parameter cannot be used in conjunction with MAXPIECESIZE. If the value of SECTION SIZE is larger than the file size, then RMAN will not use multisection backup for the file. If the section size would result in more than 256 file sections, then RMAN will increase the section size so that the result is exactly 256 sections. In the following example, the TOOLS tablespace contains a single datafile of 1 GB. The environment has two tape drives with channels allocated and the parallelism for SBT is set to two. The following command will break the tablespace datafile into two file 500MB file sections:

```
BACKUP
  SECTION SIZE 500M
  TABLESPACE tools;
```

Compressed Backups

For any use of the BACKUP command that creates backup sets, you can enable binary compression of backup sets by adding the AS COMPRESSED BACKUPSET option to the BACKUP command. RMAN will compress the backup set contents before writing to disk. Information regarding the binary compression level used is automatically recorded in the backup set. When recovering, there is no need to explicitly mention the type of compression used or how to decompress. Note that binary compression imposes a performance overhead during backup and restore operations.

It consumes CPU resources, so compressed backups should not be scheduled when CPU usage is high. An example of a command to make a compressed backup is:

```
BACKUP
AS COMPRESSED BACKUPSET
DATABASE PLUS ARCHIVELOG;
```

Encrypted Backups

RMAN allows backup sets to be created using encryption. If files of the backup sets are obtained by unauthorized users, they cannot be read or used to restore a database. Encryption can be transparent, which is based on an encryption key stored in Oracle Wallet. Alternately it can be password-based, which makes use of a user-supplied password. Dual-mode encryption combines both wallet and password-based encryption. The following commands are used to activate and modify the default encryption behavior of RMAN:

- **CONFIGURE ENCRYPTION** -- This command can be used to configure RMAN to perform transparent encryption of backup sets by default. It is not possible to persistently configure dual mode or password mode encryption.
- **SET ENCRYPTION** -- This command is used to configure dual mode or password mode encryption at the RMAN session level.

If the CONFIGURE command is used to enable transparent encryption, no additional action is required to make encrypted backups. RMAN backups will be encrypted by default. Creating a password-encrypted backup set requires the session to be specifically configured. To make password-mode encrypted backups:

1. Start RMAN and connect to a target database and recovery catalog (if used).
2. Execute the SET ENCRYPTION ON IDENTIFIED BY password ONLY command.

```
SET ENCRYPTION IDENTIFIED BY password ONLY ON FOR ALL
TABLESPACES;
```

3. Back up the database.

```
BACKUP DATABASE PLUS ARCHIVELOG;
```

Report on and maintain backups

A repository of RMAN metadata is always stored in the control file of each database on which it performs backup operations. In addition, a recovery catalog can be used to store metadata. When utilized, RMAN can store metadata for multiple target databases in a set of tables in a separate recovery catalog database. The LIST and REPORT commands provide several a number of reports to aid in determining backup actions that have been (or should be) performed..

RMAN LIST Command

The LIST command uses the information in the RMAN repository to provide lists of backups and other objects relating to backup and recovery.

- **LIST BACKUP** -- Allows you to list all backup sets, copies, and proxy copies of a database, tablespace, datafile, archived redo log, control file, or server parameter file.
- **LIST COPY** -- Allows you to list datafile copies and archived redo log files. By default, LIST COPY displays copies of all database files and archived redo logs.
- **LIST ARCHIVELOG** -- Allows you to list archive redo log files. You can list all archive log redo log files or you specify individual archive log files through SCN, time, or sequence number ranges.

- **LIST INCARNATION** -- Allows you to list all incarnations of a database. A new database incarnation is created when you open with the RESETLOGS option.
- **LIST DB_UNIQUE_NAME** -- In a Data Guard environment, each database is distinguished by its DB_UNIQUE_NAME initialization parameter setting. You can list all databases that have the same DBID.
- **LIST ... FOR DB_UNIQUE_NAME** -- Allows you to list all backups and copies for a specified database in a Data Guard environment or for all databases in the environment.
- **LIST RESTORE POINT** -- Allows you to list restore points known to the RMAN repository.
- **LIST SCRIPT NAMES** -- Allows you to list the names of recovery catalog scripts created with the CREATE SCRIPT or REPLACE SCRIPT command.
- **LIST FAILURE** -- A failure is a persistent data corruption mapped to a repair option.

List has a number of options that enables you to control how output is displayed. Some of the most common LIST options are:

- **LIST EXPIRED** -- Lists backups or copies that are recorded in the RMAN repository but that were not present at the expected location on disk or tape during the most recent crosscheck.
- **LIST ... BY FILE** -- Lists backups of each datafile, archived redo log file, control file, and server parameter file. Each row describes a backup of a file.
- **LIST ... SUMMARY** -- Provides a one-line summary of each backup.

RMAN REPORT Command

The RMAN REPORT command performs an analysis of the available backups and your database. The results of this can be used to determine actions that you should take, such as backing up specific files or removing obsolete backups to free up disk space. Some of the common uses of the REPORT command are:

- **REPORT NEED BACKUP** -- Reports which database files need to be backed up to meet a configured or specified retention policy.
- **REPORT UNRECOVERABLE** -- Reports which database files require backup because they have been affected by some NOLOGGING operation such as a direct-path INSERT.
- **REPORT OBSOLETE** -- Returns full backups, datafile copies, and archived redo logs recorded in the RMAN repository that can be deleted because they are no longer required.
- **REPORT SCHEMA** -- Returns the names of all datafiles and tablespaces for the target database at the specified point in time.

Diagnosing the Database

Set up Automatic Diagnostic Repository

Oracle 11g introduced the concept of the Automatic Diagnostic Repository (ADR). The ADR is a directory structure for diagnostic files such as traces, dumps, the alert log, health monitor reports, and more. The directory structure supports multiple instances and multiple Oracle products. Each instance of each product will store diagnostic data underneath its own home directory within the ADR. ADR provides a unified directory structure along with consistent diagnostic data formats across products and instances. This plus a unified set of tools enables diagnostic data to be correlated and analyzed across multiple Oracle products.

DIAGNOSTIC_DEST parameter

Because all diagnostic data, including the alert log, is stored in the ADR, the initialization parameters BACKGROUND_DUMP_DEST and USER_DUMP_DEST have been deprecated. They have been replaced by the initialization parameter DIAGNOSTIC_DEST. The DIAGNOSTIC_DEST parameter identifies the directory which serves as the ADR Base location

.

ADR Locations

The V$DIAG_INFO view lists all the important ADR locations for the current Oracle database instance. It also provides the number of active problems and incidents and the tracefiles for the current instance.

- **ADR Base** -- Path of ADR base
- **ADR Home** -- Path of ADR home for the current database instance
- **Diag Trace** -- Location of background process trace files, server process trace files, SQL trace files, and the text-formatted version of the alert log

- **Diag Alert** -- Location of the XML-formatted version of the alert log
- **Default Trace** -- File Path to the trace file for the current session
- **Diag Incident** -- File path for incident packages
- **Diag Cdump** -- Equivalent to cdump. Location for core dump files.
- **Health Monitor** -- Location for health monitor output.

```
SELECT name, value
FROM   v$diag_info;

NAME VALUE
--------------------- -----------------------------------------------
----
Diag Enabled          TRUE
ADR Base              /u01/oracle
ADR Home              /u01/oracle/diag/rdbms/orclbi/orclbi
Diag Trace            /u01/oracle/diag/rdbms/orclbi/orclbi/trace
Diag Alert            /u01/oracle/diag/rdbms/orclbi/orclbi/alert
Diag Incident         /u01/oracle/diag/rdbms/orclbi/orclbi/incident
Diag Cdump            /u01/oracle/diag/rdbms/orclbi/orclbi/cdump
Health Monitor        /u01/oracle/diag/rdbms/orclbi/orclbi/hm
Default Trace File
/u01/oracle/diag/rdbms/orclbi/orclbi/trace/orcl_ora_22459.trc
Active Problem Count  8
Active Incident Count 20
```

Detect database corruptions using ANALYZE and DBVERIFY

Data corruption can occur in two broad forms:

- **Intrablock** -- With this type of corruption, the problem exists within a single data block. Intrablock corruption can be either physical (i.e. the data has been physically altered on the storage media), or logical (the block is readable, but the information contained in it is logically invalid).
- **Interblock** -- Interblock corruption occurs between two or more data blocks. This type of corruption can only be logical.

Intrablock corruption is recorded in the V$DATABASE_BLOCK_CORRUPTION view. The Automatic Diagnostic Repository (ADR) tracks all types of corruptions. Many Oracle database utilities, including RMAN, can detect intrablock corruption. Interblock corruption can only be detected by the DBVERIFY utility or the ANALYZE command.

DBVERIFY

This is command-line utility that is external to the Oracle database. It is used to perform a physical data structure integrity check on database files and backup files. When run against a database file, the database can be either open or closed. DBVERIFY can only be used with data files, and is not applicable for control files or redo logs. DBVERIFY can check the disk blocks of a single data file or a specific segment.

To perform an integrity check on data file index01.dbf on Linux, run the dbv command as follows:

```
% dbv file=index01.dbf
```

To perform an integrity check on a segment, you must determine the segment id. The segment ID is composed of the tablespace ID number (tsn), segment header file number (segfile), and segment header block number (segblock). This information can be obtained from SYS_USER_SEGS. The relevant columns are TABLESPACE_ID, HEADER_FILE, and HEADER_BLOCK. To scan a segment 3.1.14, run the dbv command as follows:

```
% dbv segment_id=3.1.14
```

Reference the Oracle 11g Utilities manual for more information on the DBVERIFY utility.

ANALYZE

The SQL statement ANALYZE can be used to validate the structure of an index or index partition, table or table partition, index-organized table, cluster, or object reference. To enable this capability, the VALIDATE STRUCTURE clause must be specified. ANALYZE will check the integrity of each of the data blocks in a table or index. If corruption is detected in the structure of the object, then an error message is returned.

Detect database corruptions using the dbms_repair package

The DBMS_REPAIR package contains a number of procedures designed to detect and repair corrupt blocks in tables and indexes. The package enables administrators to address corruptions where possible. DBMS_REPAIR requires two administration tables that will be used to store a list of corrupt blocks and any index keys pointing to those blocks. The tables are created via the ADMIN_TABLES procedure:

```
BEGIN
  DBMS_REPAIR.ADMIN_TABLES (
      table_name => 'DR_REPAIR_TABLE',
      table_type => DBMS_REPAIR.repair_table,
      action     => DBMS_REPAIR.create_action,
      tablespace => 'USERS');

  DBMS_REPAIR.ADMIN_TABLES (
      table_name => 'DR_ORPHAN_TABLE',
      table_type => DBMS_REPAIR.orphan_table,
      action     => DBMS_REPAIR.create_action,
      tablespace => 'USERS');
END;
```

Once the administration tables exist, the CHECK_OBJECT procedure can be used to diagnose the suspect table for corrupt blocks:

```
DECLARE
  v_corr_blocks    NUMBER  := 0;
BEGIN
  DBMS_REPAIR.check_object (
     schema_name         => 'OCGURU',
     object_name         => 'EMPLOYEES',
     repair_table_name => 'DR_REPAIR_TABLE',
     corrupt_count       =>  v_corr_blocks);
  DBMS_OUTPUT.PUT_LINE('Corrupt block count: ' ||
TO_CHAR(v_corr_blocks));
END;
```

Implement the DB_BLOCK_CHECKING parameter to detect corruptions

The initialization parameter DB_BLOCK_CHECKING is used to specify whether or not Oracle will perform block checking for database blocks. When enabled, Oracle will go through the data in a block, ensuring that it is logically self-consistent. This check can often prevent memory and data corruption. However, performing the check can incur a 1% to 10% overhead in reading the block. The specific overhead depends on the database workload and the parameter value used. Oracle recommends setting the DB_BLOCK_CHECKING parameter to FULL if the performance overhead is acceptable. The valid values for the parameter are:

- **OFF** -- No block checking is performed for blocks in user tablespaces. However, semantic block checking for SYSTEM tablespace blocks is always turned on. For backward compatibility, a value of FALSE will be treated as OFF.
- **LOW** -- Basic block header checks are performed after block contents change in memory (for example, after UPDATE or INSERT statements, on-disk reads, or inter-instance block transfers in Oracle RAC).

- **MEDIUM** -- All LOW checks and full semantic checks are performed for all objects except indexes (whose contents can be reconstructed by a drop and rebuild on encountering a corruption).
- **FULL** -- All LOW and MEDIUM checks and full semantic checks are performed for all objects. For backward compatibility, a value of TRUE will be treated as FULL.

Repair corruptions using RMAN

Block media recovery allows you to recover individual corrupt data blocks within a data file. It is faster than data file media recovery because only blocks that need recovery are restored and recovered. Also, unlike data file media recovery, the affected data files remain online during the recovery process. Prior to the block media recovery capability, a single corrupt block in a datafile required taking the data file offline and restoring from backup.

When the database encounters a corrupt block, it marks the block as media corrupt and then writes it to disk. After being marked corrupt, no subsequent read of the block will be successful until the block is recovered. If block corruption has been detected, block media recovery can be performed manually using the RECOVER ... BLOCK command. By default, RMAN first searches for good blocks in the real-time query physical standby database (if one exists), then flashback logs and then blocks in full or level 0 incremental backups.

All known corrupted block in the database can be located by querying the V$DATABASE_BLOCK_CORRUPTION view. It contains blocks marked corrupt by database components such as RMAN, ANALYZE, dbv, and SQL queries. The following types of corruption result in the addition of rows to this view:

- **Physical corruption** -- Physical corruption, also known as media corruption, means that the database does not recognize the block: the checksum is invalid, the block contains all zeros, or the block header is corrupt. Physical corruption checking is enabled by default. Checksum checking can be disabled by specifying the NOCHECKSUM option of the BACKUP command, but other physical consistency checks cannot be disabled.
- **Logical corruption** -- Logical corruption occurs when the block has a valid checksum, the header and footer match, and so on, but the contents are logically inconsistent. Logical corruption cannot always be corrected by block media recovery. It may be necessary to use alternate recovery methods, such as tablespace point-in-time recovery, or dropping and re-creating the affected objects. Logical corruption checking is disabled by default. It can be enabled by specifying the CHECK LOGICAL option of the BACKUP, RESTORE, RECOVER, and VALIDATE commands.

The following prerequisites apply to the RECOVER ... BLOCK command:

- The target database must run in ARCHIVELOG mode and be open or mounted with a current control file.
- If the target database is a standby database, then it must be in a consistent state, recovery cannot be in session, and the backup must be older than the corrupted file.
- The backups of the data files containing the corrupt blocks must be full or level 0 backups and not proxy copies.
- RMAN can use only archived redo logs for the recovery.
- Flashback Database must be enabled on the target database for RMAN to search the flashback logs for good copies of corrupt blocks.
- The target database must be associated with a real-time query physical standby database for RMAN to search a standby database for good copies of corrupt blocks.

Recovering Individual Blocks

To recover specific data blocks, you must obtain the data file numbers and block numbers of the corrupted blocks. When Oracle encounters a corrupted block, you may get an error in a trace file like the following:

```
ORA-01578: ORACLE data block corrupted (file # 4, block # 213)
ORA-01110: data file 4: '/oracle/oradata/trgt/users01.dbf'
```

To recover this block, perform the following steps:

1. Start RMAN and connect to the target database, which must be mounted or open.
2. Run the SHOW ALL command to confirm that the appropriate channels are preconfigured.
3. Run the RECOVER ... BLOCK command at the RMAN prompt, specifying the file and block numbers for the corrupted blocks.

   ```
   RECOVER DATAFILE 4 BLOCK 213;
   ```

Recovering All Blocks in V$DATABASE_BLOCK_CORRUPTION

Rather than recovering blocks individually, you can have RMAN automatically recover all blocks listed in the V$DATABASE_BLOCK_CORRUPTION view. The steps to do this are:

1. Start SQL*Plus and connect to the target database.
2. Query V$DATABASE_BLOCK_CORRUPTION to determine whether corrupt blocks exist.

   ```
   SELECT * FROM V$DATABASE_BLOCK_CORRUPTION;
   ```

3. Start RMAN and connect to the target database.
4. Recover all blocks marked corrupt in V$DATABASE_BLOCK_CORRUPTION.

   ```
   RMAN> RECOVER CORRUPTION LIST;
   ```

Once recovered, the blocks will automatically be removed from the view.

Using RMAN to Perform Recovery

Perform complete recovery from a critical or noncritical data file loss using RMAN

The scope of performing a complete database recovery is huge and depends on dozens of factors. However, the exam is not going to get into an incredibly complex recovery scenario. This section makes the following assumptions:

- Some or all data files have been lost, but the database has not lost all current control files or an entire online redo log group.
- The database is using the current server parameter file.
- The complete set of archived redo logs and incremental backups needed for recovery of the data file backups are available. Every data file either has a backup, or a complete set of online and archived redo logs goes back to the creation of a data file with no backup.
- An encrypted tablespace is not part of the recovery.
- The database runs in a single-instance configuration.
- The database uses a fast recovery area.

Prior to starting the recovery, you should ideally perform all of the following steps:

- Identify the Database Files to Restore or Recover
- Determine the DBID of the Database
- Preview Backups Used in Restore Operations
- Validate Backups Before Restoring Them
- Restore Archived Redo Logs Needed for Recovery

To restore and recover the whole database:

- Start RMAN and connect to a target database.

```
% rman
RMAN> CONNECT TARGET /
```

- If the database is not mounted, then mount but do not open the database.

```
STARTUP MOUNT;
```

- Use the SHOW command to see which channels are preconfigured.

```
SHOW ALL;
```

  If the necessary devices and channels are already configured, then no action is necessary. Otherwise, you can use the CONFIGURE command to configure automatic channels, or include ALLOCATE CHANNEL commands within a RUN block.

- Restore and recover the database.

```
RMAN> RESTORE DATABASE;
Starting restore at 20-JAN-13
.
.
.
Finished restore at 20-JAN-13

RMAN> RECOVER DATABASE;

Starting recover at 20-JAN-13
.
.
.
media recovery complete, elapsed time: 00:00:21
Finished recover at 20-JAN-13
```

- Examine the output to see if media recovery was successful. If so, open the database.

```
ALTER DATABASE OPEN;
```

Perform incomplete recovery using RMAN

Incomplete recovery of a database, also known as Database Point-In-Time recovery (DBPITR) restores a database to a time earlier than the one that is the target time. It then uses incremental backups and/or redo to roll the database forward until the target point is reached. It is possible to recover to a specific time, SCN, log sequence number, or restore point. Creating restore points at important times is recommended to make PITR easier if it is required. If it is possible to perform a Flashback Database operation to the desired point, then this is a considerably easier option than performing DBPITR through media recovery. In order to perform DBPITR, the following pre-requisites must be met:

- The database must be running in ARCHIVELOG mode.
- There must be backups of all data files from before the target SCN and archived logs for the period between the SCN of the backups and the target SCN.

When performing DBPITR, setting the target time using the SET UNTIL command at the beginning of the procedure reduces the potential for problems. Specifying the UNTIL clause on the RESTORE and RECOVER commands individually has the potential to restore backups that are not early enough to be used in the RECOVER operation. The DBPITR example below makes the following assumptions:

- The DBPITR is being performed within the current database incarnation.
- The control file is current.
- The database is using the current server parameter file.

Performing an Incomplete Recovery:

1. Determine the time, SCN, restore point, or log sequence that ends recovery.
2. When using a target time expression instead of a target SCN, verify the time format environment variables before invoking RMAN.
3. Connect RMAN to the target database and, if applicable, the recovery catalog database. The database should be set to MOUNT status:

```
SHUTDOWN IMMEDIATE;
STARTUP MOUNT;
```

4. Perform the following operations within a RUN block:
    - Use SET UNTIL to specify the target time, SCN, or log sequence number, or SET TO when specifyin a restore point.
    - If automatic channels are not configured, then manually allocate disk and tape channels as needed.
    - Restore and recover the database.

```
RUN
{
SET UNTIL SCN 123456;
RESTORE DATABASE;
RECOVER DATABASE;
}
```

Alternately, the SET line can use time expressions, restore points, or log sequence numbers:

```
SET UNTIL TIME '12-JAN-2014 12:00:00';
SET UNTIL SEQUENCE 4397;
SET TO RESTORE POINT fy_end;
```

5. If the operation completes with no errors, open the database read-only in SQL*Plus. Perform queries as needed to ensure that the database contains the desired information.

```
ALTER DATABASE OPEN READ ONLY;
```

6. If you are satisfied with the results, then perform one of the following actions:

a) Open the database for read/write, abandoning all changes after the target SCN. The database must be shut down, remounted, and then opened with RESETLOGS:

```
SHUTDOWN IMMEDIATE;
STARTUP MOUNT;
ALTER DATABASE OPEN RESETLOGS;
```

b) Export one or more objects from the database using Data Pump. The database can then be recovered to the current time and the objects reimported.

Recover using incrementally updated backups

The RMAN BACKUP INCREMENTAL command creates an incremental backup of a database. Incremental backups capture block-level changes to a database made after a previous incremental backup. They provide a faster means of recovering a database than using redo logs alone. There are three types of incremental backups:

- **Level 0** -- This is the starting point for an incremental backup. It backs up all blocks in the database and is identical in content to a full backup.
- **Level 1 Differential** -- This backup contains only blocks changed since the most recent incremental backup. This is the default Level 1 backup.
- **Level 1 Cumulative** -- This backup contains only blocks changed since the most recent level 0 backup.

When restoring incremental backups, RMAN uses the level 0 backup as the starting point. It then uses the level 1 backups to update changed blocks where possible to avoid reapplying changes from redo one at a time. If incremental backups are available, then RMAN uses them during recovery.

The following example creates a level 0 incremental backup to serve as a base for an incremental backup strategy:

```
BACKUP INCREMENTAL LEVEL 0 DATABASE;
```

The following example creates a level 1 cumulative incremental backup:

```
BACKUP INCREMENTAL LEVEL 1 CUMULATIVE DATABASE;
```

The following example creates a level 1 differential incremental backup:

```
BACKUP INCREMENTAL LEVEL 1 DATABASE;
```

When performing media recovery, RMAN will determine whether or not the database can be restored using an incremental backup. RMAN will always make use of incremental backups over archived redo los when recovering because it is much slower to apply redo than apply changes at a block level using incremental backups. It is not necessary to restore a base incremental backup of a data file in order to apply incremental backups. It is possible to restore data file image copies and recover them using incremental backups.

Switch to image copies for fast recovery

One option to reduce database recovery time is to use incrementally updated backups. In this strategy, an image copy of each data file is created. Periodically the image copy is rolled forward by making and applying a level 1 incremental backup. If the image files need to be used for recovery, the only redo that needs to be applied is whatever redo has been generated since the last incremental backup.

Incrementally Updating Backups

This process avoids the overhead of making full image copy backups of datafiles, while minimizing media recovery time. If incremental changes are created and applied by a daily backup script, there will never be more than 1 day of redo to apply during media recovery. After the incremental changes have been made to a given backup data file, it will be identical to the datafile at the time of the most recently applied incremental level 1 backup.

- Create a full image copy backup of a data file with a specified tag.
- At regular intervals, make a level 1 differential incremental backup of the data file with the same tag as the base data file copy.
- Apply the incremental backup to the most recent backup with the same tag.

To create incremental backups for use in an incrementally updated backups strategy, use the BACKUP ... FOR RECOVER OF COPY WITH TAG form of the BACKUP command. The script following is a very basic example of implementing a strategy based on incrementally updated backups.

```
RUN
{
  RECOVER COPY OF DATABASE
    WITH TAG 'incr_update';
  BACKUP
    INCREMENTAL LEVEL 1
    FOR RECOVER OF COPY WITH TAG 'incr_update'
    DATABASE;
}
```

Restore a database onto a new host

Restoring a backup of your existing database to a new host might be required if your current host develops hardware troubles. Alternately, you may simply be upgrading to a newer hardware platform. In any event, RMAN can be used to move your existing data to the new platform as follows:

1. Start RMAN and connect to a target database and recovery catalog.
2. Run a LIST command to see a listing of backups of the datafile and control file autobackups.

```
LIST COPY;
LIST BACKUP OF CONTROLFILE;
```

3. Copy the backups to the new host with an operating system utility.
4. Edit the /etc/group file on the new host so that you are included in the DBA group:

```
dba:*:614:<your_user_name>
```

5. Set the ORACLE_SID environment variable on the new host to the same value used on the original:

```
% setenv ORACLE_SID orclprod
```

6. Start RMAN on hostb and connect to the target database without connecting to the recovery catalog.

```
% rman NOCATALOG
RMAN> CONNECT TARGET /
```

7. Set the DBID and start the database instance without mounting the database.

```
SET DBID 423498230;
STARTUP NOMOUNT
```

8. RMAN will fail to find the server parameter file, which has not yet been restored, but will start the instance with a "dummy" file.

9. Allocate a channel to the media manager, then restore the server parameter file as a client-side parameter file and use the SET command to indicate the location of the autobackup.

```
RUN
{
ALLOCATE CHANNEL c1 DEVICE TYPE sbt PARMS '...';
SET CONTROLFILE AUTOBACKUP FORMAT FOR DEVICE TYPE DISK TO
'/tmp/%F';
RESTORE SPFILE
TO PFILE '?/oradata/test/inittrgta.ora'
FROM AUTOBACKUP;
SHUTDOWN ABORT;
}
```

10. Edit the restored initialization parameter file.
11. Change any location-specific parameters, for example, those ending in _DEST, to reflect the new directory structure.

```
IFILE
LOG_ARCHIVE_DEST_1
CONTROL_FILES
```

12. Restart the instance with the edited initialization parameter file.

```
STARTUP FORCE NOMOUNT PFILE='?/oradata/test/inittrgta.ora';
```

13. Restore the control file from an autobackup and then mount the database.

```
RUN
{
ALLOCATE CHANNEL c1 DEVICE TYPE sbt PARMS '...';
RESTORE CONTROLFILE FROM AUTOBACKUP;
ALTER DATABASE MOUNT;
}
```

14. RMAN restores the control file to whatever locations you specified in the CONTROL_FILES initialization parameter.
15. Catalog the datafile copies that you moved to the new host, using their new filenames. You can use CATALOG START WITH if the files are in directories with a common prefix:

```
CATALOG START WITH '/oracle/oradata/trgt/';
```

16. If you want to specify files individually, then you can execute a CATALOG command as follows:

```
CATALOG DATAFILECOPY
'/oracle/oradata/trgt/system01.dbf',
'/oracle/oradata/trgt/undotbs01.dbf',
'/oracle/oradata/trgt/cwmlite01.dbf',
'/oracle/oradata/trgt/drsys01.dbf',
'/oracle/oradata/trgt/example01.dbf',
'/oracle/oradata/trgt/indx01.dbf',
'/oracle/oradata/trgt/tools01.dbf',
'/oracle/oradata/trgt/users01.dbf';
```

17. Start a SQL*Plus session on the new database and query the database filenames recorded in the control file.
18. Because the control file is from the hosta database, the recorded filenames use the original hosta filenames. You can query V$ views to obtain this information. Run the following query in SQL*Plus:

```
COLUMN NAME FORMAT a60
SPOOL  LOG '/tmp/db_filenames.out'
SELECT file# AS "File/Grp#", name
FROM   v$datafile
UNION
SELECT group#, member
FROM   v$logfile;
SPOOL OFF
EXIT
```

19. Write the RMAN restore and recovery script. The script must include the following steps:
    - ✓ For each datafile on the destination host that is restored to a different path than it had on the source host, use a SET NEWNAME command to specify the new path on the destination host.
    - ✓ For each online redo log that is to be created at a different location than it had on the source host, use SQL ALTER DATABASE RENAME FILE commands to specify the pathname on the destination host.
    - ✓ Perform a SET UNTIL operation to limit recovery to the end of the archived redo logs.
    - ✓ Restore and recover the database.
    - ✓ Run the SWITCH DATAFILE ALL command so that the control file recognizes the new datafile path names.

```
RUN
{
ALLOCATE CHANNEL c1 DEVICE TYPE sbt PARMS '...';

SET NEWNAME FOR DATAFILE 1 TO
'?/oradata/test/system01.dbf';
SET NEWNAME FOR DATAFILE 2 TO
'?/oradata/test/undotbs01.dbf';
SET NEWNAME FOR DATAFILE 3 TO '?/oradata/test/indx01.dbf';
SET NEWNAME FOR DATAFILE 4 TO
'?/oradata/test/tools01.dbf';
SET NEWNAME FOR DATAFILE 5 TO
'?/oradata/test/users01.dbf';
SQL "ALTER DATABASE RENAME FILE
''/dev3/oracle/dbs/redo01.log''
TO ''?/oradata/test/redo01.log'' ";
SQL "ALTER DATABASE RENAME FILE
''/dev3/oracle/dbs/redo02.log''
TO ''?/oradata/test/redo02.log'' ";

SET UNTIL SCN 123456;
RESTORE DATABASE;
SWITCH DATAFILE ALL;

# recover the database
RECOVER DATABASE;
}
EXIT
```

20. Execute the script created in the previous step.

```
% rman TARGET / NOCATALOG
RMAN> @reco_test.rman
```

21. From the RMAN prompt, open the database with the RESETLOGS option:

```
ALTER DATABASE OPEN RESETLOGS;
```

Recover using a backup control file

In a recovery scenario where all copies of the current control file are lost or damaged, you must restore and mount a backup control file. Copy the backup control file to all of the locations listed in the CONTROL_FILES initialization parameter. After the control files are in place, the RECOVER command must be issued, even if no datafiles have been restored.

RMAN automatically searches during the recovery process for online and archived logs that are not recorded in the RMAN repository. Any that are found will be cataloged in the control file. It searches for archived redo logs in any current archiving destination that are in the log format specified in the initialization parameter file used to start the instance. RMAN will also attempt to locate the online redo logs by using the filenames listed in the control file. If the archiving destination or format has been altered during recovery, or if you added new online log members after the backup of the control file, this process may fail. In that case, RMAN may not be able to automatically catalog a needed online or archived log. If this happens, you must use the CATALOG command to manually add the required redo logs so that recovery can proceed.

The database will expect to find the control files in the locations defined in the CONTROL_FILES initialization parameter. If this parameter is not set, then the default control file location uses the rules defined in the CREATE CONTROLFILE statement. If the backup control files cannot be copied to the original locations, the CONTROL_FILES initialization parameter can be changed to reflect new locations.

Once the control files are in place and any required redo logs have been cataloged, you may recover the database with the RECOVER command:

```
RECOVER DATABASE USING BACKUP CONTROLFILE UNTIL CANCEL;
```

Once the restore operation has been completed, open the database with the RESETLOGS option.

Perform Disaster recovery

Disaster recovery assumes that the entire database has been lost, including all datafiles, the recovery catalog database, all current control files, all online redo log files, and all parameter files. Recovering the database in the event of a loss like this requires:

- Backups of all datafiles
- All archived redo logs generated after the creation time of the oldest backup that you intend to restore
- At least one control file autobackup
- A record of the DBID of the database

In this recovery, it is assumed that the server hardware the database was on has been damaged beyond repair. A full backup exists and the Oracle software has been installed on a new host with the same directory structure. The four requirements listed above have been met.

To recover the database on the new host:

1. If possible, restore or re-create all relevant network files such as tnsnames.ora and listener.ora and a password file.
2. Start RMAN and connect to the target database instance using operating system authentication.

```
RMAN> CONNECT TARGET /
```

3. Specify the DBID for the target database with the SET DBID command.

```
SET DBID 343487540;
```

4. Issue the STARTUP NOMOUNT command.
5. Allocate a channel to the media manager and then restore the server parameter file from autobackup.

```
RUN
{
ALLOCATE CHANNEL c1 DEVICE TYPE sbt;
RESTORE SPFILE FROM AUTOBACKUP;
}
```

6. Restart the instance with the restored server parameter file.

```
STARTUP FORCE NOMOUNT;
```

7. Write a command file to perform the restore and recovery operation, and then execute the command file. The command file should do the following:
   - ✓ Allocate a channel to the media manager.
   - ✓ Restore a control file autobackup.
   - ✓ Mount the restored control file.
   - ✓ Catalog any backups not recorded in the repository with the CATALOG command.
   - ✓ Restore the datafiles to their original locations.
   - ✓ Recover the datafiles. RMAN stops recovery when it reaches the log sequence number specified.

```
RMAN> RUN
{
ALLOCATE CHANNEL t1 DEVICE TYPE sbt;
RESTORE CONTROLFILE FROM AUTOBACKUP;
ALTER DATABASE MOUNT;
RESTORE DATABASE;
RECOVER DATABASE;
}
```

8. If recovery was successful, then open the database and reset the online logs:

```
ALTER DATABASE OPEN RESETLOGS;
```

Performing Tablespace Point-in-Time Recovery

Identify the situations that require TSPITR

TSPITR stands for Tablespace Point-In-Time Recovery. Recovery Manager TSPITR enables you to recover one or more tablespaces in a database to an earlier time. Unlike incomplete recovery TSPITR can be performed without affecting the rest of the tablespaces and objects in the database. TSPITR is useful in several situations:

- Recovering a logical database to a point different from the rest of the physical database, when multiple logical databases exist in separate tablespaces of one physical database.
- Recovering data lost after data definition language (DDL) operations that change the structure of tables.
- Recovering a table after it has been dropped with the PURGE option.
- Recovering from the logical corruption of a table.
- Recovering dropped tablespaces.

Perform automated TSPITR

RMAN TSPITR is complex enough that I highly recommend reading the "Performing RMAN Tablespace Point-in-Time Recovery (TSPITR)" chapter in the Oracle Database Backup and Recovery User's Guide. While this section of the study guide will cover the test topic as listed on the Oracle Education site, if you don't really understand TSPITR, you will not have the background to really perform this function. Also, depending on how the questions are worded in the test, you may not have sufficient context to answer them.

To perform fully automated RMAN TSPITR, the user performing the operation should be able to connect as SYSDBA using operating system authentication. The AUXILIARY DESTINATION parameter is used to set a location for RMAN to use for the auxiliary set data files. The auxiliary destination must be a location on disk with enough space to hold auxiliary set data files.

1. Start an RMAN session on the target database and, if applicable, connect to a recovery catalog.
2. Configure any channels required for TSPITR on the target instance.
3. Run the RECOVER TABLESPACE command, specifying both the UNTIL clause and the AUXILIARY DESTINATION parameter.

```
RECOVER TABLESPACE users, tools
UNTIL LOGSEQ 1700 THREAD 1
AUXILIARY DESTINATION '/u01/auxdest';
```

4. If TSPITR completes successfully, then back up the recovered tablespace before bringing it online. After you perform TSPITR on a tablespace, you can no longer use previous backups of that tablespace.
5. Bring the tablespace back online.

```
RMAN> SQL "ALTER TABLESPACE users, tools ONLINE";
```

Using Flashback Technology

Restore dropped tables from the recycle bin

By default, when a table is dropped, the database does not immediately remove the space associated with the table. Instead, the database renames it and places the table and any associated objects that were dropped in a recycle bin. If it is determined that the table was dropped in error, it can be recovered at a later date. The FLASHBACK TABLE statement is used to restore the table.

The recycle bin is a data dictionary table that contains information required to recover dropped objects. The dropped objects themselves remain where they were before being dropped and still occupy the same amount of disk space. Dropped objects also continue to count against user space quotas until they are explicitly purged or are purged by the database due to tablespace space constraints.

When a tablespace including its contents is dropped, the recycle bin does not come into play. The storage where the objects were does not exist any more. The database purges any entries in the recycle bin for objects that were located in the tablespace. If the recycle bin is disabled, dropped tables and their dependent objects are not placed in the recycle bin; they are just dropped. They must be recovered by other means, such as recovering from backup. The recycle bin is enabled by default.

The FLASHBACK TABLE ... TO BEFORE DROP statement is used to recover objects from the recycle bin. When recovering a table, you must specify either the system-generated name of the table in the recycle bin or the original table name. An optional RENAME TO clause lets you rename the table as you recover it. The USER_RECYCLEBIN view can be used to obtain the system-generated name. To use the FLASHBACK TABLE ... TO BEFORE DROP statement, you need the same privileges required to drop the table.

The following example restores ocp_employees table and assigns to it a new name:

```
FLASHBACK TABLE ocp_employees TO BEFORE DROP
RENAME TO ocp_employees_take2;
```

Perform Flashback Query

Oracle Flashback Query allows a prior time to be specified when executing a query against the database. The query will return results as they would have appeared at that time. This can be used to recover from an unwanted change in the recent past by selecting a target time before the error and executing a query to retrieve the lost or damaged data.

The Oracle Flashback Query capability is implemented via the AS OF clause in a SELECT statement. When the AS OF clause is included, Oracle retrieves data as it existed at an earlier point in time. The AS OF clause must explicitly reference a past time through a time stamp or System Change Number (SCN). When a timestamp is used, the time will be accurate to within three seconds. If greater accuracy is required, an SCN should be utilized. The query will return committed data that was current at the specified time/SCN. The following example retrieves the row for employee with the ID 107 at an earlier point in time:

```
SELECT *
FROM   hr.employees
AS OF TIMESTAMP
    TO_TIMESTAMP('2014-03-14 12:30:00', 'YYYY-MM-DD HH:MI:SS')
WHERE employee_id = 107;
```

If that record had been accidentally deleted from the table, it could be recovered with the following statement:

```
INSERT INTO hr.employees
(SELECT *
 FROM   hr.employees
 AS OF TIMESTAMP
     TO_TIMESTAMP('2014-03-14 12:30:00', 'YYYY-MM-DD HH:MI:SS')
 WHERE employee_id = 107);
```

Use Flashback Transaction

Oracle Flashback Transaction allows a transaction to be reversed. Oracle will determine the dependencies between transactions and create a compensating transaction to reverse the unwanted change. The result is a state as if the transaction and any dependent transactions had never happened.

A Flashback Transaction Query is used to retrieve metadata and historical data for a single transaction or for all transactions in a supplied interval. The data is generated from the static data dictionary view FLASHBACK_TRANSACTION_QUERY. The Flashback Transaction Query creates a column UNDO_SQL. The SQL text in this field is the logical opposite of the DML operation performed by the transaction shown. The code from this field can usually reverse the original transaction within reason (e.g. a SQL_UNDO INSERT operation would be unlikely to insert a row back at the same ROWID from which it was deleted). As a general rule, Oracle Flashback Transaction Query is used in conjunction with an Oracle Flashback Version Query that provides transaction IDs.

```
SELECT operation, start_scn, commit_scn, logon_user
  FROM flashback_transaction_query
    WHERE xid = HEXTORAW('09000900A9010000');

OPERATION    START_SCN COMMIT_SCN LOGON_USER
------------ --------- ---------- ------------
UNKNOWN         393394     393463 OCPGURU
BEGIN           393394     393463 OCPGURU
```

The following statement uses Oracle Flashback Version Query as a subquery to associate each row version with the LOGON_USER responsible for the row data change.

```
SELECT xid, logon_user
  FROM flashback_transaction_query
    WHERE xid IN (
      SELECT versions_xid
      FROM employees VERSIONS BETWEEN TIMESTAMP
        TO_TIMESTAMP('22-FEB-14 11.40.00 PM',
                     'DD-MON-YY HH:MI:SS AM') AND
        TO_TIMESTAMP('22-FEB-14 11.56.00 PM',
                     'DD-MON-YY HH:MI:SS AM')
       );
```

You can use the DBMS_FLASHBACK.TRANSACTION_BACKOUT procedure to roll back a transaction and its dependent transactions while the database remains online. Transaction backout uses undo data to create and execute the compensating transactions to return the affected data to its original state. TRANSACTION_BACKOUT does not commit the DML operations that it performs as part of transaction backout. However, it does hold all the required locks on rows and tables in the right form to prevent other dependencies from entering the system. To make the transaction backout permanent, you must explicitly commit the transaction.

In order to configure a database for the Oracle Flashback Transaction Query feature, the database must be running in ARCHIVELOG mode. In addition, the database administrator must enable supplemental logging.

```
ALTER DATABASE ADD SUPPLEMENTAL LOG DATA;
```

To perform Oracle Flashback Query operations, the administrator must grant appropriate privileges to the user who will be performing them. For Oracle Flashback Query, the administrator can do either of the following:

- To allow access to specific objects during queries, grant FLASHBACK and SELECT privileges on those objects.
- To allow queries on all tables, grant the FLASHBACK ANY TABLE privilege.

For Oracle Flashback Transaction Query, the administrator will need to grant the SELECT ANY TRANSACTION privilege. To allow execution of undo SQL code retrieved by an Oracle Flashback Transaction, the administrator will need to grant: SELECT, UPDATE, DELETE, and INSERT privileges for the appropriate tables. Finally, the administrator will need to grant the user EXECUTE privileges on the DBMS_FLASHBACK Package.

Additional Flashback Operations

Perform Flashback Table operations

By default, when a table is dropped, the database does not immediately remove the space associated with it. Instead, the database renames the object in the data dictionary and places the table and any associated objects that were dropped into a recycle bin. If it is determined that the table was dropped in error, it can be recovered at a later date. The FLASHBACK TABLE statement is used to restore a table.

The recycle bin is a data dictionary table that contains information required to recover dropped objects. The dropped objects themselves remain where they were before being dropped and still occupy the same amount of disk space. Dropped objects also continue to count against user space quotas until they are explicitly purged or are purged by the database due to tablespace space constraints.

When a tablespace including its contents is dropped, the recycle bin does not come into play. The storage where the objects were does not exist anymore. The database purges any entries in the recycle bin for objects that were located in the tablespace. If the recycle bin is disabled, dropped tables and their dependent objects are not placed in the recycle bin; they are just dropped. They must be recovered by other means, such as recovering from backup. The recycle bin is enabled by default.

The FLASHBACK TABLE ... TO BEFORE DROP statement is used to recover objects from the recycle bin. When recovering a table, you must specify either the system-generated name of the table in the recycle bin or the original table name. An optional RENAME TO clause lets you rename the table as you recover it. The USER_RECYCLEBIN view can be used to obtain the system-generated name. To use the FLASHBACK TABLE ... TO BEFORE DROP statement, you need the same privileges required to drop the table.

The following example restores ocp_employees table and assigns to it a new name:

```
FLASHBACK TABLE ocp_employees TO BEFORE DROP
RENAME TO ocp_employees_take2;
```

Configure, Monitor Flashback Database and Perform Flashback Database operations

Oracle's Flashback Database feature allows you to set the database back to an earlier time in order to correct problems caused by logical data corruption or user errors within a designated time window. Flashback Database is much more efficient than performing a point-in-time recovery and does not require a backup and restore operation. Flashback Database is accessible through the RMAN command FLASHBACK DATABASE or the SQL statement FLASHBACK DATABASE.

To enable Flashback Database, the database must have a Fast Recovery Area configured and a flashback retention target set. This target specifies how far in the past it should possible to rewind the database. Flashback Database uses its own logging mechanism, creating flashback logs and storing them in the fast recovery area. The database must be set up in advance to create flashback logs in order to take advantage of this feature. Once configured, at regular intervals, the database copies images of each altered block in every data file into the flashback logs. These block images can later be used to reconstruct the data file contents to any moment for which logs exist. In addition to the flashback logs, redo logs on disk or tape must be available for the entire time period spanned by the flashback logs. The range of SCNs for which there is currently enough flashback log data to support the FLASHBACK DATABASE command is called the flashback database window.

If the Fast Recovery Area does not contain sufficient space for recovery files such as archived redo logs and other backups needed for the retention policy, the database may delete the flashback logs starting from the earliest SCNs. The flashback retention target does not guarantee that Flashback Database is available for the full period. A larger Fast Recovery Area may be required in this case.

Flashback Database has the following limitations:

- It can only undo changes to a data file made by Oracle Database. It cannot be used to repair media failures, or recover from accidental deletion of data files.
- It cannot undo a shrink data file operation.
- If the database control file is restored from backup or re-created, all accumulated flashback log information is discarded.
- If you Flashback Database to a target time at which a NOLOGGING operation was in progress, block corruption is likely in the database objects and datafiles affected by the NOLOGGING operation.

A normal restore point simply assigns a restore point name to an SCN or specific point in time. It functions as an alias for this SCN. If you use flashback features or point-in-time recovery, the restore point name can be used instead of a time or SCN. Normal restore points eventually age out of the control file if not manually deleted, so they require no ongoing maintenance. The following commands support the use of restore points:

- RECOVER DATABASE and FLASHBACK DATABASE commands in RMAN
- FLASHBACK TABLE statement in SQL

A guaranteed restore point also serves as an alias for an SCN in recovery operations. However, guaranteed restore points never age out of the control file and must be explicitly dropped. It ensures that you can use Flashback Database to rewind a database to the restore point SCN, even if the generation of flashback logs is not enabled. When enabled, a guaranteed restore point enforces the retention of flashback logs all the way back in time to the guaranteed SCN.

In order to enable Flashback Database, you must first ensure the database instance is open or mounted. If the instance is mounted, then the database must be shut down cleanly unless it is a physical standby database.

1. Optionally, set the DB_FLASHBACK_RETENTION_TARGET to the length of the desired flashback window in minutes. The default is 1 day (1440 minutes).
2. Enable the Flashback Database feature for the whole database:

   ```
   ALTER DATABASE FLASHBACK ON;
   ```

3. Optionally, disable flashback logging for specific tablespaces.

To disable Flashback Database logging, you must issue the following command on a database instance that is either in mount or open state:

```
ALTER DATABASE FLASHBACK OFF;
```

Maintaining flashback logs does not impose significant overhead on a database instance. Changed blocks are written to the flashback logs at relatively infrequent, regular intervals, to limit processing and I/O overhead. Optimizing performance is primarily a matter of ensuring that the writes occur as fast as possible.

- Use a fast file system for your fast recovery area, preferably without operating system file caching.
- Configure enough disk spindles for the file system that holds the fast recovery area.
- If the storage system used to hold the fast recovery area does not have nonvolatile RAM, then try to configure the file system on striped storage volumes with a relatively small stripe size such as 128 KB.
- For large databases, set the initialization parameter LOG_BUFFER to at least 8 MB.

There are several database views that allow you to monitor the impact of flashback logs on the database. The V$FLASHBACK_DATABASE_LOG view allows you to monitor the Flashback Database retention target and how much space is being used by the flashback logs in the Fast Recovery Area.

- **OLDEST_FLASHBACK_SCN** -- Lowest system change number (SCN) in the flashback data, for any incarnation.
- **OLDEST_FLASHBACK_TIME** -- Time of the lowest SCN in the flashback data, for any incarnation.
- **RETENTION_TARGET** -- Target retention time (in minutes).
- **FLASHBACK_SIZE** -- Current size (in bytes) of the flashback data.
- **ESTIMATED_FLASHBACK_SIZE** -- Estimated size of flashback data needed for the current target retention.

The V$FLASHBACK_DATABASE_STAT view displays statistics for monitoring the I/O overhead of logging flashback data. It also displays the estimated flashback space needed based on previous workloads.

- **BEGIN_TIME** -- Beginning of the time interval.
- **END_TIME** -- End of the time interval.
- **FLASHBACK_DATA** -- Number of bytes of flashback data written during the interval.
- **DB_DATA** -- Number of bytes of database data read and written during the interval.
- **REDO_DATA** -- Number of bytes of redo data written during the interval.
- **ESTIMATED_FLASHBACK_SIZE** -- Value of ESTIMATED_FLASHBACK_SIZE in V$FLASHBACK_DATABASE_LOG at the end of the time interval.

The V$RECOVERY_FILE_DEST view displays information about the disk quota and current disk usage in the fast recovery area.

- **NAME** -- Location name. This is the value specified in the DB_RECOVERY_FILE_DEST initialization parameter.

- **SPACE_LIMIT** -- Maximum amount of disk space (in bytes) that the database can use for the fast recovery area. This is the value specified in the DB_RECOVERY_FILE_DEST_SIZE initialization parameter.
- **SPACE_USED** -- Amount of disk space (in bytes) used by fast recovery area files created in current and all previous fast recovery areas. Changing fast recovery areas does not reset SPACE_USED to 0.
- **SPACE_RECLAIMABLE** -- Total amount of disk space (in bytes) that can be created by deleting obsolete, redundant, and other low priority files from the fast recovery area.
- **NUMBER_OF_FILES** -- Number of files in the fast recovery area.

Set up and use a Flashback Data Archive

Oracle's Flashback Data Archive feature allows you to store table-level change history for extended periods of time. It provides the ability to track all transactional changes to a table over its lifetime. The Flashback Data Archive functionality is useful to maintain compliance with record storage policies and audit reports. It is possible to have multiple Flashback Data Archives in a single database, one of which can be (although it is not required), specified as the default for the database. Each Flashback Data Archive in a database is configured with a retention time that determines how long data stored in that particular archive is to be retained.

Flashback archiving is off for any table by default. You can enable flashback archiving for a table if all of the following are true:

- You have the FLASHBACK ARCHIVE object privilege on the Flashback Data Archive that you want to use for that table.
- The table you want to archive is not nested, clustered, temporary, remote, or external.
- The table does not contain LONG or nested columns.

Once flashback archiving is enabled for a table, you can disable it only if you either have the FLASHBACK ARCHIVE ADMINISTER system privilege or you are logged into the database with SYSDBA privileges. While flashback archiving is enabled for a table, some DDL statements are not allowed on it and will generate an ORA-55610 error. The following operations are disallowed:

- ALTER TABLE statement that includes an UPGRADE TABLE clause, with or without an INCLUDING DATA clause
- ALTER TABLE statement that moves or exchanges a partition or subpartition operation
- DROP TABLE statement

Flashback Data Archive can be the solution to any number of business requirements. Many government agencies and organizations require that data be kept for a set number of years before being deleted. The settings of a Flashback Data Archive can be specifically configured to meet these requirements. After the specified time period has expired, the data will automatically be aged out of the archive – effectively 'shredding' it without requiring direct intervention. It can help in satisfying some of the storage requirements for such legislative acts as Sarbanes-Oxley and HIPAA. It can provide a source of data for audits. Flashback data archive can also be used as a simple method to recover accidentally altered or deleted data.

A Flashback Data Archive is created using the CREATE FLASHBACK ARCHIVE statement. If you are logged on with SYSDBA privileges, you can also specify that this is the default Flashback Data Archive for the system. When creating a new flashback data archive, you must specify the following:

- Name of the Flashback Data Archive
- Name of the first tablespace of the Flashback Data Archive
- Retention time (number of days that Flashback Data Archive data for the table is guaranteed to be stored)

- (Optional) Maximum amount of space that the Flashback Data Archive can use in the first tablespace. The default is unlimited.

Create a default Flashback Data Archive named fda1 using a maximum of 15 Gigs of tablespace fda_tbs1. The data will be retained for two years:

```
CREATE FLASHBACK ARCHIVE DEFAULT fda1
TABLESPACE fda_tbs1 QUOTA 15G RETENTION 2 YEAR;
```

Create a Flashback Data Archive named fda2 that uses tablespace fda_tbs2, whose data will be retained for three years:

```
CREATE FLASHBACK ARCHIVE fda2
TABLESPACE fda_tbs2 RETENTION 3 YEAR;
```

Using the ALTER FLASHBACK ARCHIVE statement, you can change the retention time of a Flashback Data Archive; purge some or all of its data; and add, modify, or remove tablespaces. If you are logged on with SYSDBA privileges, you can also make a specific archive the default Flashback Data Archive for the system.

- Make Flashback Data Archive fla1 the default Flashback Data Archive:

  ```
  ALTER FLASHBACK ARCHIVE fda1 SET DEFAULT;
  ```

- Add an additional 5Gigs quota of tablespace fda_tbs1 to Flashback Data Archive fda1:

  ```
  ALTER FLASHBACK ARCHIVE fda1
  ADD TABLESPACE da_tbs1 QUOTA 5G;
  ```

- Add unlimited quota on tablespace fda_tbs3 to Flashback Data Archive fda1:

  ```
  ALTER FLASHBACK ARCHIVE fda1 ADD TABLESPACE tbs3;
  ```

- Change the retention time for Flashback Data Archive fda1 to four years:

```
ALTER FLASHBACK ARCHIVE fda1 MODIFY RETENTION 4 YEAR;
```

- Purge all historical data older than one day from Flashback Data Archive fda1:

```
ALTER FLASHBACK ARCHIVE fda1
PURGE BEFORE TIMESTAMP (SYSTIMESTAMP - INTERVAL '1' DAY);
```

You can drop a Flashback Data Archive with the DROP FLASHBACK ARCHIVE statement. This statement will delete its historical data, but will not drop the tablespace the archive was stored on. To remove Flashback Data Archive fda1 and all its historical data:

```
DROP FLASHBACK ARCHIVE fda1;
```

Flashback archiving is disabled for all tables by default. If a flashback data archive exists in the database, and you have the FLASHBACK ARCHIVE privilege on it, you can enable flashback archiving for a table. To enable flashback archiving for a table, you use the FLASHBACK ARCHIVE clause in either a CREATE TABLE or ALTER TABLE statement. It's possible to set the specific Flashback Data Archive where the data for the table will be stored in the FLASHBACK ARCHIVE clause. If no clause is provided, the default Flashback Data Archive for the database will be used. Some examples of making tables use flashback archiving are:

- Create table dept and use the default Flashback Data Archive:

```
CREATE TABLE dept (DEPTNO NUMBER(4) NOT NULL,
                   DEPTNAME VARCHAR2(10))
FLASHBACK ARCHIVE;
```

- Create table employee and use the Flashback Data Archive fda1:

```
CREATE TABLE dept (DEPTNO NUMBER(4) NOT NULL,
                   DEPTNAME VARCHAR2(10))
FLASHBACK ARCHIVE fda1;
```

- Enable flashback archiving for the table dept and use the default Flashback Data Archive:

```
ALTER TABLE dept FLASHBACK ARCHIVE;
```

- Enable flashback archiving for the table dept and use the Flashback Data Archive fda1:

```
ALTER TABLE dept FLASHBACK ARCHIVE fda1;
```

- Disable flashback archiving for the table dept:

```
ALTER TABLE dept NO FLASHBACK ARCHIVE;
```

The following views in the data dictionary are specific to the Flashback Data Archive:

- DBA_FLASHBACK_ARCHIVE_TABLES
- DBA_FLASHBACK_ARCHIVE
- DBA_FLASHBACK_ARCHIVE_TS

Transport Data and Tablespaces

Describe the concepts of transportable tablespaces and databases

It is possible to transport tablespaces between servers using RMAN's transport tablespace capability. The RMAN TRANSPORT TABLESPACE command will create a transportable tablespace set. This set contains data files for a one or more tablespaces plus an export file that contains the structural metadata for included tablespaces. The export file is generated by Data Pump Export rather than by RMAN. The RMAN TRANSPORT TABLESPACE command does not require access to the live data files from the tablespaces to be transported. It creates the tablespace set from database backups. It is also possible to specify a target point in time, SCN, or restore point for the set to be exported so long at that time exists within the recovery window.

In order to create a tablespace set with the TRANSPORT TABLESPACE operation, a backup of all needed tablespaces and archived redo log files must be accessible to RMAN. The transport process occurs in the following steps:

1. RMAN starts an auxiliary instance on the same host as the source database. This instance is used to perform the restore and recovery of the tablespaces.
2. RMAN restores a backup of the source database control file to serve as the auxiliary instance control file.
3. RMAN restores auxiliary set and transportable set data files from the backups of the source database. The auxiliary set includes files that are required for the tablespace transport but which are not part of the transportable tablespace set. It typically includes the SYSTEM and SYSAUX tablespaces, temp files, and data files containing rollback or undo segments.
4. RMAN performs database point-in-time recovery (DBPITR) at the auxiliary instance as of the target time specified for the TRANSPORT TABLESPACE command. When a target time is not specified, the recovery uses all available redo.
5. RMAN opens the auxiliary database with the RESETLOGS options.

6. RMAN places the transportable set tablespaces of the auxiliary instance into read-only mode. It then executes Data Pump Export in transportable tablespace mode to create the export dump file for the transportable set.
7. If the preceding steps are successful, then RMAN shuts down the auxiliary instance and deletes all files created during the operation except for the transportable set files, the Data Pump Export file, and the sample import script.

The following limitations apply to transporting tablespaces:

- The source and the destination databases must use compatible database character sets.
- The destination database cannot contain a tablespace of the same name. If it does, you must rename either the tablespace to be transported or the one in the destination database.
- Objects with underlying objects (such as materialized views) or contained objects (such as partitioned tables) are not transportable unless all of the underlying or contained objects are in the tablespace being transported.
- Transportable tablespaces cannot transport tables with TIMESTAMP WITH TIMEZONE (TSTZ) data across platforms with different time zone file versions.
- Transportable tablespaces cannot transport encrypted tablespaces or tablespaces containing tables with encrypted columns.
- Administrative tablespaces, such as SYSTEM and SYSAUX, cannot be included in a transportable tablespace set.
- Tablespaces that do not use block encryption but that contain tables with encrypted columns cannot be transported.

Transporting databases

When transporting a database to a different platform, both must have the same endian format. The process of moving a database between platforms can be largely automated through the RMAN CONVERT DATABASE command. After the transport operation, the new database will contain the same data as the original and most of the same settings. The CONVERT DATABASE command will automatically transport the following files to the destination platform:

- Data files for permanent tablespaces
- Initialization parameter file

The format of the data files can be converted either on the source or destination platforms. When the CONVERT DATABASE ON DESTINATION PLATFORM command is used, RMAN does not convert the data files. Instead, RMAN generates scripts to run on the destination platform in order to perform the conversion. Two parameters control the creation of additional scripts:

- **CONVERT SCRIPT** -- Creates a script to be executed on the destination host to convert data file copies in batch mode.
- **TRANSPORT SCRIPT** -- Generates a script that contains SQL statements to create the new database on the destination platform.

Transport tablespaces across different platforms

It is possible to transport tablespaces from an Oracle database on one platform to an Oracle database on a different platform. If the source and destination platforms have the same endian format, it is possible to simply copy the associated files from one platform to the other using operating system commands. The RMAN CONVERT command is required when transporting tablespaces when the endian formats are different between the source and destination platforms. If the entire database is being moved, even if the platforms have the same endian format, any data files with undo information must be converted using RMAN.

Tablespace conversion is performed using the RMAN CONVERT TABLESPACE command on the **source** host only. The command will generate output files in the correct format for the destination platform.

The data files in the source database are not altered by the CONVERT command.

The RMAN CONVERT DATAFILE command can be used to convert files on the **destination** host only. Because the data files are not associated with any given tablespace on the destination, individual files must be specified by name in RMAN.

The list of available platforms and their respective endian formats are available from the V$TRANSPORTABLE_TABLESPACE view:

```
SELECT platform_id, platform_name, endian_format
FROM   v$transportable_platform
WHERE  platform_name LIKE '%Linux%';

PLATFORM_ID PLATFORM_NAME                  ENDIAN_FORMAT
----------- ------------------------------ --------------
         10 Linux IA (32-bit)              Little
         11 Linux IA (64-bit)              Little
          9 IBM zSeries Based Linux        Big
         13 Linux x86 64-bit               Little
         18 IBM Power Based Linux          Big
```

Using RMAN to Duplicate a Database

Creating a duplicate database

There are two basic types of duplication: active database duplication and backup-based duplication. When backup-based duplication is performed, it can be performed with or without a target or recovery catalog connection. When performing active database duplication, connections to both a target and a recovery catalog are required.

Active Database Duplication

When performing active database duplication, RMAN connects as TARGET to the source database instance and as AUXILIARY to the auxiliary instance. The source database is copied over the network to the auxiliary instance. This option requires no backups of the source database. The files required can be copied by RMAN in one of two ways:

- **Image Copies** -- Once RMAN establishes a connection to the source database, the source database will transfer the database files to the auxiliary database. This is referred to as the push-based method of active database duplication and may require additional resources on the source database. RMAN only uses image copies when no auxiliary channels are allocated or when the number of auxiliary channels allocated is less than the number of target channels.
- **Backup Sets** -- RMAN establishes a connection to the source database and the auxiliary database. The auxiliary will connect to the source database through Oracle Net Services and retrieve the files from the source database. This is referred to as the pull-based method. When backup sets are used, RMAN can employ unused block compression while creating backups. This can reduce the size of the backups being transported over the network. Using this method, it is also possible to create the backup sets in parallel using multisection backups and/or encrypt backup sets as they are created. RMAN uses backup sets to

perform active database duplication when the connection to the target database is established using a net service name and one of the following conditions is satisfied:

- The DUPLICATE ... FROM ACTIVE DATABASE command contains either the USING BACKUPSET, USING COMPRESSED BACKUPSET, or SECTION SIZE clause.
- The number of auxiliary channels allocated is equal to or greater than the number of target channels allocated.

Backup-Based Duplication

When backup-based duplication is utilized, the duplicate database makes use of preexisting RMAN backups and copies. Backup-based duplication can be performed via one of three methods. The method used determines where RMAN obtains the metadata about the backups.

- **No target database connection** -- The metadata is pulled from a recovery catalog.
- **No target database connection or recovery catalog** -- The metadata about where backups and copies reside is supplied in the BACKUP LOCATION clause of the DUPLICATE command.
- **With a target database connection** -- The metadata about backups is pulled from the target database control file or from the recovery catalog.

Using a duplicate database

When a new database is created via the RMAN DUPLICATE command, all of the data (or a subset) in the source database is copied to a new set of data files. The duplicated database is entirely independent from the source database once the DUPLICATE operation has been completed. A database created in this fashion can be used for several purposes:

- Testing backup and recovery procedures.
- Testing an upgrade to a new release of Oracle Database.
- Testing the effect of applications on database performance.
- Creating a standby database.
- Generating reports without using resources on the production database.

When a database is copied using operating system utilities, the DBID will remain the same as the original. Before the copied database can be registered in the same recovery catalog as the original, the DBID must be changed using the DBNEWID utility. When the DUPLICATE command is used, it automatically assigns the duplicate database a new DBID. The copy can be registered in the same recovery catalog as the source database as-is.

Monitoring and Tuning RMAN

Monitoring RMAN sessions and jobs

It is possible to monitor the progress of RMAN backups and restore jobs by querying the V$SESSION_LONGOPS view. V$SESSION_LONGOPS contains detail rows and aggregate rows on RMAN operations. The detail rows are most useful in determining the progress of each backup set.

- **Detail rows** -- These rows describe the files being processed by a single job step. A job step is the creation or restoration of one backup set or data file copy. Detail rows are updated with every buffer that is read or written during the backup step.
- **Aggregate rows** -- These rows describe the files processed by all job steps in an RMAN command. They are updated when each job step completes, so their granularity of update is large.

V$SESSION_LONGOPS Columns Relevant for RMAN

- **SID** -- The server session ID corresponding to an RMAN channel
- **SERIAL#** -- The server session serial number.
- **OPNAME** -- A text description of the row. Examples of details rows include “RMAN: datafile copy”, “RMAN: full datafile backup”, and “RMAN: full datafile restore”. “RMAN: aggregate input” and “RMAN: aggregate output” are the only aggregate rows.
- **CONTEXT** -- For backup output rows, this value is 2. For all other rows except proxy copy (which does not update this column), the value is 1.
- **SOFAR** -- The meaning of this column depends on the type of operation described by this row:
  - ✓ For image copies, the number of blocks that have been read
  - ✓ For backup input rows, the number of blocks that have been read from the files being backed up
  - ✓ For backup output rows, the number of blocks that have been written to the backup piece
  - ✓ For restores, the number of blocks that have been processed to the files that are being restored in this one job step
  - ✓ For proxy copies, the number of files that have been copied

- **TOTALWORK** -- The meaning of this column depends on the type of operation described by this row:
  - ✓ For image copies, the total number of blocks in the file.
  - ✓ For backup input rows, the total number of blocks to be read from all files processed in this job step.
  - ✓ For backup output rows, the value is 0 because RMAN does not know how many blocks that it will write into any backup piece.
  - ✓ For restores, the total number of blocks in all files restored in this job step.
  - ✓ For proxy copies, the total number of files to be copied in this job step.

A script designed to query V$SESSION_LONGOPS would be similar to the following:

```
SELECT sid, serial#, context, sofar, totalwork,
       ROUND(sofar/totalwork*100,2) "%_COMPLETE"
FROM   v$session_longops
WHERE  opname LIKE 'RMAN%'
AND    opname NOT LIKE '%aggregate%'
AND    totalwork != 0
AND    sofar <> totalwork;
```

Tuning RMAN

RATE

The RMAN commands ALLOCATE and CONFIGURE CHANNEL both have a RATE parameter. This is used to specify the bytes per second that are read on a channel. It is intended to set an upper limit for bytes read in order to prevent RMAN from consuming excessive disk bandwidth. This ensures that there is disk bandwidth available for other database operations. If the backup is not streaming to tape, the RATE parameter should not be set.

Large Pool

RMAN is one of the several users of the large pool. The total size of the pool must be sufficient for all the processes that use it. This is especially true if the DBWR_IO_SLAVES parameter has been set. The value of the LARGE_POOL_SIZE initialization parameter should be set or increased if the database reports an error in the alert log stating that there is insufficient memory to start I/O slaves. The error message will be similar to the following:

```
ksfqxcre: failure to allocate shared memory means sync I/O will be
used whenever async I/O to file not supported natively
```

To set the large pool size:

1. Start SQL*Plus and connect to the target database.
2. Set the LARGE_POOL_SIZE initialization parameter in the target database.
3. The ALTER SYSTEM SET statement can be used to set the parameter dynamically.
4. ALTER SYSTEM SET LARGE_POOL_SIZE = 512M scope=both;
5. Restart the RMAN backup.

Multiplexing

When performing an incremental backup, RMAN will only back up blocks that have changed since a previous backup that is part of the same strategy. If block change tracking is not enabled, RMAN must scan the entire data file for changed blocks. The changed blocks are written to output buffers as RMAN finds them. If relatively few blocks changed while RMAN is making an SBT backup, the output buffers may not fill fast enough to keep the tape drive streaming. In these cases, it is possible to improve backup performance by adjusting the level of multiplexing. This is the number of input files that are simultaneously read and written to the same RMAN backup piece. The level of multiplexing determined by the smaller of the number of input files placed in each backup set and the MAXOPENFILES setting on the channel.

Tuning the Copy and Write Phases

There are several options for tuning the Copy and Write phases depending on the circumstances. Some alternatives for improving this are:

- If the performance issue is with a full backup, consider using incremental backups. Incremental level 1 backups write only the changed blocks from data files to tape. If there is a bottleneck when writing to tape, this will reduce the impact on the overall backup strategy.
- For backups that use the basic compression algorithm, consider using the Advanced Compression Option.
- On a database host with multiple CPUs and a backup using binary compression, try increasing the number of channels.
- For an encrypted backup, change the encryption to AES128, which is the least CPU-intensive algorithm.
- If RMAN is backing up files to ASM, then increase the number of channels up to a maximum of 16.

You can use the DURATION parameter of the BACKUP command to limit the amount of time a given backup job is given to run. To specify a backup duration:

```
BACKUP
DURATION 4:00
TABLESPACE users;
```

The above command will generate an error if the backup does not complete inside the window. If the keyword PARTIAL is specified, RMAN does not report an error but rather displays a message showing which files are not backed up. If the BACKUP command is part of a RUN block, then the remaining commands in the RUN block continue to execute.

Specifying FILESPERSET of 1 will save each file as its own backup set. If the window closes before the backup is complete, only the current set (one file) is lost. The following example prevents RMAN from issuing an error and minimizes lost work when a backup partially completes:

```
BACKUP
DURATION 4:00 PARTIAL
TABLESPACE users
FILESPERSET 1;
```

Minimizing Backup Load and Duration

When using DURATION you can run the backup with the maximum possible performance, or run as slowly as possible while still finishing within the allotted time, to minimize the performance impact of backup tasks. To maximize performance, use the MINIMIZE TIME option with DURATION.

```
BACKUP
DURATION 4:00 PARTIAL
MINIMIZE TIME
DATABASE
FILESPERSET 1;
```

When MINIMIZE LOAD is specified, RMAN monitors the progress of the running backup, and periodically estimates how long the backup will take to complete at its present rate. If RMAN estimates that the backup will finish before the end of the backup window, then it slows down the rate of backup so that the full available duration is used. This reduces the overhead on the database associated with the backup. To extend the backup to use the full time available, use the MINIMIZE LOAD option:

```
BACKUP
DURATION 4:00 PARTIAL
MINIMIZE LOAD
DATABASE
FILESPERSET 1;
```

Configure RMAN for Asynchronous I/O

When an RMAN channel accesses a disk for read or write operations, the I/O is either synchronous or asynchronous. When performing synchronous I/O, a server process can perform only one task at a time. When using asynchronous I/O, a server process can begin an I/O operation and then perform some other task while waiting for the I/O to complete. It is also possible to start additional I/O operations without having to wait for the first to complete. When reading from an ASM disk group, you should use asynchronous disk I/O if possible.

Disk I/O Slaves

Many operating systems support asynchronous I/O natively. If an operating system does not support native asynchronous I/O, the database can use special I/O slave processes to simulate it. The availability of disk I/O slaves is controlled by setting the DBWR_IO_SLAVES initialization parameter. By default, the value is 0 and I/O server processes are not used. Set DBWR_IO_SLAVES to enable RMAN to perform asynchronous I/O if and only if your disk does not support asynchronous I/O natively. Any nonzero value for DBWR_IO_SLAVES causes a fixed number of disk I/O slaves to be used for backup and restore, which simulates asynchronous I/O. To enable disk I/O slaves:

1. Start SQL*Plus and connect to the target database.
2. Shut down the database.
3. Set DBWR_IO_SLAVES initialization parameter to a nonzero value.
4. Restart the database.

Tape I/O Slaves

The initialization parameter BACKUP_TAPE_IO_SLAVES specifies whether or not RMAN uses slave processes. Tape devices can only be accessed by a single process at one time, so RMAN uses only the number of slaves necessary for the number of tape devices. If set to true, RMAN will allocate tape buffers from the SGA. When the LARGE_POOL_SIZE initialization parameter is also set, then RMAN allocates buffers from the large pool. When BACKUP_TAPE_IO_SLAVES is set to false, RMAN allocates tape buffers from the PGA. When making use of I/O slaves, set the LARGE_POOL_SIZE initialization parameter to dedicate space for these large memory allocations. This prevents RMAN I/O buffers from competing with the library cache for SGA memory.

Database Architecture and ASM

Describe Automatic Storage Management (ASM)

Oracle Automatic Storage Management (ASM) is a storage solution for Oracle Database files. It acts as a volume manager to provide a file system for the exclusive use of the database. When using ASM, partitioned disks are assigned to ASM with specifications for striping and mirroring. When making use of Automatic Storage Management, in addition to any database instances that exist, there will be an instance dedicated to ASM. Oracle ASM also makes use of the Oracle Managed Files (OMF) feature. OMF automatically creates files in the locations designated, as well as naming them. It also removes the files automatically when tablespaces or files are deleted from within Oracle. The ASM instance exists to manage the disk space and distribute the I/O load across multiple drives to optimize performance. ASM provides several benefits over using standard data files:

- Simplifies operations such as creating databases and managing disk space
- Distributes data across physical disks to provide uniform performance
- Rebalances data automatically after storage configuration changes

An Oracle ASM instance uses the same basic technology as an Oracle Database instance. The System Global Area (SGA) and background processes of an ASM instance are similar to those of Oracle Database. The SGA for an ASM instance is much smaller than a database instance and has fewer internal components because the ASM instance has fewer functions. The only function of an ASM instance is to mount disk groups and make the associated file available to database instances. There is no database instance mounted by Oracle ASM instances. The logical storage elements of an Oracle ASM instance are:

- **ASM Disks** -- A storage device that is provisioned to an Oracle ASM disk group. It can be a physical disk or partition, a Logical Unit Number (LUN) from a storage array, a logical volume, or a network-attached file.
- **ASM Disk Groups** -- A collection of Oracle ASM disks managed as a logical unit.
- **ASM Files** -- A file stored in an Oracle ASM disk group. The database can store data files, control files, online redo log files, and other types of files as Oracle ASM files.
- **ASM Extents** -- The raw storage used to hold the contents of an Oracle ASM file. An ASM file consists of one or more file extents and an ASM extent consists of one or more ASM allocation units.
- **ASM Allocation Units** -- The fundamental unit of allocation within a disk group.
- **ASM Instances** -- A special Oracle instance that manages Oracle ASM disks. They manage the metadata of the disk group and provide file layout information to the database instances.

Oracle ASM supports the majority of file types required by the database. The list below shows the most commonly used file types and default template that provides the attributes for file creation. Oracle ASM cannot directly support some administrative file types on disk groups. These include trace files, audit files, alert logs, export files, and core files.

- **Control files** -- CONTROLFILE
- **Data files** -- DATAFILE
- **Redo log files** -- ONLINELOG
- **Archive log files** -- ARCHIVELOG
- **Temporary files** -- TEMPFILE
- **Data file backup pieces** -- BACKUPSET
- **Archive log backup piece** -- BACKUPSET
- **Persistent initialization parameter file (SPFILE)** -- PARAMETERFILE
- **Flashback logs** -- FLASHBACK
- **Data Pump dumpset** -- DUMPSET

Fully Qualified File Name Form

Whenever a file is created in ASM, Oracle Managed Files automatically generates a fully qualified file name for it. The fully qualified filename represents a complete path name in the Oracle ASM file system. You can use a fully qualified file name for referencing existing Oracle ASM files in Oracle ASM operations, except for disk group creation. A fully qualified file name has the following form:

+diskgroup/dbname/filetype/filetypetag.file.incarnation.

The definitions of the individual elements are:

- **+diskgroup** -- The disk group name preceded by a plus sign. The plus sign (+) is equivalent to the root directory for the Oracle ASM file system.
- **dbname** -- The DB_UNIQUE_NAME of the database to which the file belongs.
- **filetype** -- The Oracle file type and can be one of the file types shown in Table 7–3.
- **filetypetag** -- Type-specific information about the file.
- **file.incarnation** -- The file/incarnation pair, used to ensure uniqueness.

An example of a fully qualified Oracle ASM filename is:

+data/ocpdb/controlfile/Current.221.46544321

The file creation request does not specify the fully qualified filename. It supplies an alias or just a disk group name. Oracle ASM then creates the file in the correct Oracle ASM path based on the file type. ASM then assigns an appropriate fully qualified filename. If an alias is specified in the creation request, ASM creates the alias and points it to the fully qualified filename. ASM file creation requests are either single or multiple file creation requests.

Alias Filenames

Alias filenames can be used for referencing existing files and creating new ASM files. Alias names consist of the disk group name preceded by a plus sign followed by a name string. Alias filenames use a hierarchical directory structure, with the slash (/) or backslash (\) character separating name components. Aliases must include the disk group name. They cannot exist at the root level (+). When a file is created with an alias, both the alias and fully-qualified names are recorded and you can access the file with either name. Alias filenames do not (and cannot) end in a dotted pair of numbers. Examples of alias filenames include:

- +data/ocpdb/control_file_main
- +data/ocpdb/control_file_bkup
- +fra/recover/second.dbf

The example below creates an undo tablespace with a data file that has an alias name, and with attributes that are set by the user-defined template my_undo_template. This example assumes that the **ocpdb** directory has been created in disk group **data**.

```
CREATE UNDO TABLESPACE ocpundo
DATAFILE '+data/ocpdb/ocp_undo_ts' SIZE 200M;
```

If an alias is used to create the data file, it is not an Oracle Managed Files (OMF) file. This means that the file will not be automatically deleted when the tablespace is dropped. To drop the file manually after the tablespace has been dropped, use the following SQL statement:

```
ALTER DISKGROUP data DROP FILE '+data/ocpdb/ocp_undo_ts';
```

Set up initialization parameter files for ASM and database instances

When an Oracle instance starts, it makes use of an initialization parameter file to determine many of the database settings that will be used. At minimum, this file must specify the DB_NAME parameter. If the file contains nothing else, all other parameters will be set to default values. There are two types of parameter file that Oracle can use: a text-based parameter file that is read-only to the Oracle instance (PFILE), or a binary file that the instance can both read from and write to (SPFILE). When an instance stats, Oracle uses the following steps to locate an initialization parameter file. It will use the first file it locates:

1. It looks for spfile[SID].ora
2. It looks for spfile.ora
3. It looks for init[SID].ora

The recommended option is to utilize the binary file. It is called a server parameter file or spfile. Unlike the other options, with a spfile, you can change initialization parameters using ALTER SYSTEM commands and have those changes persist across a database shutdown and startup. The spfile also provides a method by which Oracle can self-tune. A spfile can be created manually from your text-based initialization file. Alternately, DBCA can automatically generate one when the database is created. When a server parameter file does not exist, the instance will start using a text initialization parameter file. At startup, the instance initially searches for a server parameter file in a default location. Only if it does not find one will the instance will search for a text initialization parameter file. It's also possible to bypass an existing server parameter file by naming a PFILE as a STARTUP argument.

The default file name for the text initialization parameter file is init[SID].ora. For a database with a SID of oraprod, the default filename would be initoraprod.ora. The default location under Unix and Linux is in the ORACLE_HOME/dbs directory. Under MS Windows, the file would be stored in ORACLE_HOME\database by default.

Many of the database initialization parameters can be dynamically changed using the ALTER SYSTEM statement. For instances using a spfile, such changes can persist across shutdowns. However, if you are using a text initialization parameter file, any changes made via ALTER SYSTEM are effective only for the current instance. You must update them manually in the initialization parameter file to make them permanent.

The text initialization parameter file contains name/value pairs in one of the following forms:

- **Single-Value Parameters** – parameter_name=value
- **Multiple-Value Parameters** – parameter_name=(value[,value] ...)

Multiple-value parameters can also be entered on multiple lines using the same format as a single parameter. If a single-value parameter appears on more than one line in the file, only the last value will be used.

Some initialization parameters derive their values from the values of other parameters. As a general rule, the values for derived parameters should not be altered. However, if they are explicitly set, then the specified value will override the calculated value. An example of a derived parameter is SESSIONS. This parameter is calculated from the value of the PROCESSES parameter. Unless SESSIONS is set explicitly, when the value of PROCESSES changes, then the default value of SESSIONS changes as well.

The host operating system will determine the valid values or value ranges of some initialization parameters. The DB_BLOCK_BUFFERS parameter indicates the number of data buffers in main memory. The maximum allowable value for this parameter depends on the operating system. In addition, the size of data block buffers, set by DB_BLOCK_SIZE, defaults to 8K under most operating systems.

Common Initialization Parameters

The following are all commonly set initialization parameters. These and other initialization parameters are listed in more detail in the Oracle 11g Reference Manual.

- **DB_NAME** – Determines the local component of the database name.
- **DB_DOMAIN** – Indicates the domain (logical location) within a network structure. This parameter is optional. The combination of the DB_NAME and DB_DOMAIN must create a database name that is unique within a network.
- **CONTROL_FILES** – Specifies one or more control filenames for the database. Control files are generated at the time a database is created using the names specified by the CONTROL_FILES parameter. If you do not include CONTROL_FILES in the initialization parameter file, Oracle will create a control file in the same directory as the initialization parameter file, using a default operating system–dependent filename.
- **PROCESSES** – Determines the maximum number of OS processes that can connect to Oracle simultaneously. At minimum, this parameter must have a minimum value of one for each background process plus one for each user process.
- **MEMORY_TARGET** – Sets a target memory size for the instance. The total memory used by the instance will remain reasonably constant, based on the supplied value. The instance will automatically distribute memory between the system global area (SGA) and the instance program global area (instance PGA).
- **SGA_TARGET** – If MEMORY_TARGET is not set, you can enable the automatic shared memory management feature by setting the SGA_TARGET parameter to a nonzero value. This parameter sets the total size of the SGA. Oracle will automatically tune the SGA components as needed.

- **SGA_MAX_SIZE** – Specifies the maximum size of the System Global Area for the lifetime of the instance. If you do not specify SGA_MAX_SIZE, then Oracle Database selects a default value that is the sum of all components specified or defaulted at the time of initialization.
- **PGA_AGGREGATE_TARGET** – Allows you to control the total amount of memory dedicated to the instance PGA.
- **UNDO_MANAGEMENT** – When set to AUTO or null, this parameter enables automatic undo management. When set to MANUAL, undo management will use manual mode.
- **UNDO_TABLESPACE** – This parameter is optional, and valid only in automatic undo management mode. The parameter specifies the name of an undo tablespace. It is used only when the database has multiple undo tablespaces.
- **DB_BLOCK_SIZE** – Sets the standard block size for the database. The standard block size is used for the SYSTEM tablespace and will be used for other tablespaces by default. Oracle can support up to four additional nonstandard block sizes.
- **COMPATIBLE** – Used to make Oracle act as if it were an earlier release of the software.
- **DIAGNOSTIC_DEST** – Used to determine the location of the Automatic Diagnostic Repository.
- **LOG_ARCHIVE_DEST_n** – Determines where to write Archived Redo Logs.
- **OPEN_CURSORS** – Sets the maximum number of open cursors for an individual session.
- **SESSIONS** – Sets the maximum number of sessions that can connect to the database.

Displaying Database Parameters

You can determine the values of instance parameters in from either SQL*Plus or SQL Developer. Parameter values can be determined by querying the V$PARAMETER view:

```
SELECT name, value
FROM   v$parameter
WHERE  name LIKE '%size%';

NAME                           VALUE
------------------------------ -----------
sga_max_size                   1073741824
shared_pool_size               0
large_pool_size                0
java_pool_size                 0
streams_pool_size              0
shared_pool_reserved_size      18454937
java_max_sessionspace_size     0
db_block_size                  8192
```

You can also use the “show parameter” command to display one or more parameters. The parameter name given in the command is treated as a wildcard. Any parameters for which the supplied value is a part of the name will be displayed:

```
show parameter pool_size

NAME                         TYPE        VALUE
---------------------------- ----------- -----
global_context_pool_size     string
java_pool_size               big integer 0
large_pool_size              big integer 0
olap_page_pool_size          big integer 0
shared_pool_size             big integer 0
streams_pool_size            big integer 0
```

If you give a complete parameter name, only the one parameter will be returned:

```
show parameter large_pool_size

NAME                         TYPE        VALUE
---------------------------- ----------- -----
large_pool_size              big integer 0
```

You can use the "show spparameter" command to view parameter values that have been specified in the server parameter file. Since there is nothing in the value column below, the parameter value has not been specified in the file:

```
show spparameter shared_pool_reserved_size

SID NAME                      TYPE        VALUE
--- ------------------------- ----------- ------
*   shared_pool_reserved_size big integer
```

The following database views can be used to locate information about database parameters.

- **V$PARAMETER** – Displays the values of initialization parameters in effect for the current session.
- **V$PARAMETER2** – Similar to V$PARAMETER. However it is easier to distinguish list parameter values in this view because each list parameter value appears in a separate row.
- **V$SYSTEM_PARAMETER** – Displays the values of initialization parameters in effect for the instance.
- **V$SPPARAMETER** – Displays the current contents of the SPFILE. It returns FALSE values in the ISSPECIFIED column if an SPFILE is not being used by the instance.

Altering Initialization Parameter Values

There are two broad classes of initialization parameters: static and dynamic. Static parameters affect the entire database and can only be modified by changing the PFILE or SPFILE and require a database shutdown before they will take effect. Dynamic parameters can be altered while the instance is running and will take effect without requiring a shutdown. Dynamic parameters can be further subdivided into session and system-level parameters:

- **Session-level parameters** – Affect only a single session. These can be altered using the ALTER SESSION command and will only affect the session in which that command is executed. The changed values expire as soon as that session is closed.
- **System-level parameters** – Affect the entire database and all sessions. They can be set with the ALTER SYSTEM command and can either be temporary or permanent.

You can use the ALTER SYSTEM statement with the SET clause to alter initialization parameter values. When doing so, there is a second optional SCOPE clause that determines the scope of the change. For instances that are not using a server parameter file, only the SCOPE=MEMORY is a valid option. Permanent parameter changes will have to be made by manually altering the text-based parameter file.

- **SCOPE = SPFILE** – The change is applied in the server parameter file only. No change is made to the current instance. The change is effective at the next startup and is persistent. This scope can be used with either static or dynamic parameters.
- **SCOPE = MEMORY** – The change is applied in memory only. The change is made to the current instance and is effective immediately. The change is not persistent because the server parameter file is not updated. This scope is only valid for dynamic parameters.
- **SCOPE = BOTH** – The change is applied in both the server parameter file and memory. The change is made to the current instance and is effective immediately. The effect is persistent because the server parameter file is updated. This scope is only valid for dynamic parameters.

There are two more optional modifiers that add additional functionality to the ALTER SYSTEM command:

- **COMMENT** – For instances using a server parameter file, this clause can be used with the SPFILE and BOTH options to add a comment to the SPFILE along with the changed parameter (i.e. 'Changed on 4/28/2012 by Matt Morris').

- **DEFERRED** – This keyword is valid for dynamic parameters with the MEMORY and BOTH options for parameters that are session-specific. The change will be made effective only for future sessions.

ASM Initialization Parameters

When installing Oracle ASM in a standalone configuration, Oracle Universal Installer creates a server parameter file for the Oracle ASM instance. The ASM SPFILE is stored in a disk group during installation. For a clustered Oracle ASM environment, OUI creates a single, shared SPFILE for Oracle ASM in a disk group. It's possible to use an SPFILE or a text-based initialization parameter file (PFILE) as the Oracle ASM instance parameter file. Oracle recommends that the Oracle ASM SPFILE is placed in a disk group.

You can set ASM parameters using the Oracle ASM Configuration Assistant (ASMCA). Some parameters can be set after database creation using Oracle Enterprise Manager or SQL ALTER SYSTEM or ALTER SESSION statements. The Oracle ASM* parameters use suitable defaults for most environments. Any parameters that have names prefixed with Oracle ASM* cannot be used in database instance parameter files. There are several database initialization parameters that are also valid for an Oracle ASM instance and the default values for these are appropriate in most cases. Some of parameters for ASM instances are:

- **ASM_DISKGROUPS** -- Specifies a list of disk groups that an Oracle ASM instance mounts at startup. The default value of the ASM_DISKGROUPS parameter is a NULL string.
- **ASM_DISKSTRING** -- Specifies a comma-delimited list of strings that limits the set of disks that an Oracle ASM instance discovers. The discovery strings can include wildcard characters.
- **ASM_POWER_LIMIT** -- Specifies the default power for disk rebalancing in a disk group. The range of values is 0 to 1024. The default value is 1. A value of 0 disables rebalancing.

- **ASM_PREFERRED_READ_FAILURE_GROUPS** -- Specifies the failure groups that should be preferentially read by the given instance. Generally used for clustered Oracle ASM instances and its value can be different on different nodes.
- **DB_CACHE_SIZE** -- Determines the size of the buffer cache. Not required when using automatic memory management.
- **DIAGNOSTIC_DEST** -- Specifies the directory where diagnostics for an instance are located. The default value is the $ORACLE_BASE directory.
- **INSTANCE_TYPE** -- Set to ASM for an ASM instance.
- **LARGE_POOL_SIZE** -- Specifies the size of the LARGE_POOL memory area. Not required when using automatic memory management.
- **PROCESSES** -- This parameter affects Oracle ASM, but the default value is usually suitable.
- **SHARED_POOL_SIZE** -- Determines the amount of memory required to manage the instance. The setting for this parameter is also used to determine the amount of space that is allocated for extent storage. Not required when using automatic memory management.

Start up and shut down ASM instances

An Oracle ASM instance is started much like an Oracle database instance with some minor differences. When starting an Oracle ASM instance, note the following:

You must set the ORACLE_SID environment variable to the Oracle ASM system identifier (SID). The default Oracle ASM SID for a single-instance database is +ASM, and the default SID for Oracle ASM for an Oracle RAC node is +ASMnode_number where node_number is the number of the node. The ORACLE_HOME environment variable must be set to the Grid Infrastructure home where Oracle ASM was installed.

- The initialization parameter file must contain the following entry: INSTANCE_TYPE = ASM. This indicates that it is an Oracle ASM instance rather than a database instance.
- When you run the STARTUP command, rather than trying to mount and open a database, this command attempts to mount Oracle ASM disk groups.

An ASM instance interprets SQL*Plus STARTUP command parameters differently than a database instance.

- **FORCE** -- Issues a SHUTDOWN ABORT to the Oracle ASM instance before restarting it.
- **MOUNT or OPEN** -- Mounts the disk groups specified in the ASM_DISKGROUPS initialization parameter. This is the default. An OPEN state for an ASM instance doesn't really exist. If supplied, this parameter is simply treated as MOUNT.
- **NOMOUNT** -- Starts up the Oracle ASM instance without mounting any disk groups.
- **RESTRICT** -- Starts up an instance in restricted mode. Only users with both the CREATE SESSION and RESTRICTED SESSION system privileges can connect.

The SYSASM operating system privilege and the OSASM operating system group allow storage responsibilities to be assigned to System Administrators without granting high-level access to the Oracle database itself. Users can be created in the ASM instance and granted the SYSASM privilege. This allows them to connect to the ASM instance and perform administration tasks. Similarly, assigning an operating system user to the OSASM group would allow then to connect as SYSASM using OS authentication.

```
$ export ORACLE_SID=+ASM
$ sqlplus / as sysasm

CREATE USER asm_admin IDENTIFIED by badpassword_nobiscuit;
User created.
```

```
SQL> GRANT SYSASM TO asm_admin;


SQLPLUS /NOLOG
SQL> CONNECT asm_admin AS SYSASM
Enter password: badpassword_nobiscuit
Connected to an idle instance.

SQL> STARTUP
ASM instance started
Total System Global Area 71303168 bytes
Fixed Size 1069292 bytes
Variable Size 45068052 bytes
ASM Cache 25165824 bytes
ASM disk groups mounted
```

Shutting Down an Oracle ASM Instance

An ASM instance is shut down using the SHUTDOWN command in SQL*Plus just as with a database instance. As with startup, you must ensure that the ORACLE_SID environment variable is set to the Oracle ASM SID before connecting to SQL*Plus. Before you shut down an ASM instance, you should shut down all database instances that use it. You should also dismount all file systems mounted on Oracle ASM Dynamic Volume Manager volumes before attempting to shut down the ASM instance.

To shut down an Oracle ASM instance, perform the following steps:

```
SQLPLUS /NOLOG
SQL> CONNECT asm_admin AS SYSASM
Enter password: badpassword_nobiscuit
Connected.
SQL> SHUTDOWN NORMAL
```

The SHUTDOWN modes when used with an Oracle ASM instance are:

- **NORMAL** -- The instance waits for any in-progress SQL to complete before dismounting all of the disk groups and shutting down. The instance also waits for all currently connected users to disconnect from the instance. If any database instances are connected to the ASM instance, then the SHUTDOWN command aborts and returns an error. NORMAL is the default mode.
- **IMMEDIATE or TRANSACTIONAL** -- The instance waits for any in-progress SQL to complete before dismounting all of the disk groups and shutting down the Oracle ASM instance. It does not wait for users currently connected to the instance to disconnect. If any database instances are connected to the Oracle ASM instance, then the SHUTDOWN aborts with an error. ASM instances have no transactions, so TRANSACTIONAL and IMMEDIATE are equivalent.
- **ABORT** -- The instance immediately shuts down without the orderly dismount of disk groups. This requires recovery on the next Oracle ASM startup. Any database instances that are connected to the Oracle ASM instance will also perform a shutdown abort because their storage will no longer be available.

Administer ASM disk groups

An ASM disk group consists of multiple disks and is the fundamental object that Oracle ASM manages. Disk groups contain the information required to manage drive space. The sub-components of disk groups include disks, files, and allocation units. A given file is contained within a single disk group. However, a disk group can contain files from several databases. A single database can use files from multiple disk groups.

Disk Group Attributes

Disk group attributes are parameters that are bound to a disk group rather than an Oracle ASM instance. Some of the more common attributes are below. Refer to the Oracle ASM Administrator's Guide for more details.

- **ACCESS_CONTROL.ENABLED** -- This attribute determines whether Oracle ASM File Access Control is enabled for a disk group. The value can be true or false. The default is false. This attribute can only be set when altering a disk group.
- **ACCESS_CONTROL.UMASK** -- This attribute determines which permissions are masked out on the creation of an Oracle ASM file for the user that owns the file, users in the same user group, and others not in the user group. This attribute applies to all files on a disk group.
- **AU_SIZE** -- A file extent consists of one or more allocation units. An Oracle ASM file consists of one or more file extents. When you create a disk group, you can set the Oracle ASM allocation unit size with the AU_SIZE disk group attribute. The values can be 1, 2, 4, 8, 16, 32, or 64 MB, depending on the specific disk group compatibility level.
- **COMPATIBLE.ASM** -- This attribute controls the format of data structures for ASM metadata in the given disk group. The ASM software version must be equal or greater than this value in order to be able to access the disk group. The COMPATIBLE.ASM attribute must always be greater than or equal to COMPATIBLE.RDBMS for the same disk group. For example, you can set COMPATIBLE.ASM for the disk group to 11.0 and COMPATIBLE.RDBMS for the disk group to 10.1. In this case, the disk group can be managed only by ASM software with a version of 11.0 or higher. However, any database client of version 10.1 or higher can use the disk group. If you will be increasing both parameters, the COMPATIBLE.ASM value must be increased first.
- **COMPATIBLE.RDBMS** -- This dictates the format of messages that are exchanged between the Automatic Storage Management instance and the database instance. This parameter set the minimum database client release that may access a given disk group. You can set different values of this parameter on diskgroups within the same ASM instance for multiple database clients running at different compatibility settings.

- **CONTENT.TYPE** -- Identifies the disk group type: data, recovery, or system. The type value determines the distance to the nearest neighbor disk in the failure group where Oracle ASM mirrors copies of the data. The default value is 'data' which specifies a distance of 1 to the nearest neighbor disk. A value of 'recovery' specifies a distance of 3 to the nearest neighbor disk and a value of 'system' specifies a distance of 5.
- **DISK_REPAIR_TIME** -- Determines the amount of time that a disk can be unavailable due to a transient failure before to being dropped permanently from the diskgroup. To use this parameter, both the compatible.rdbms and compatible.asm attributes must be set to at least 11.1. You cannot set this attribute when creating a disk group, but you can alter the DISK_REPAIR_TIME attribute in an ALTER DISKGROUP ... SET ATTRIBUTE statement to change the default value. If both compatible.rdbms and compatible.asm are set to at least 11.1, then the default is 3.6 hours. If either parameter is less than 11.1, the disk is dropped immediately if it becomes inaccessible. The time can be specified in units of minutes by using the letter M or hours by using the letter H. If you provide a number with no unit, then the default is hours. The default attribute value can be changed while bringing the disk offline by using an ALTER DISKGROUP ... DISK OFFLINE statement and the DROP AFTER clause. If a disk is taken offline using the current value of DISK_REPAIR_TIME, and the value of this attribute for the diskgroup is subsequently changed with the ALTER DISKGROUP ... SET ATTRIBUTE statement, then the changed value is used by ASM in determining when to drop the disk.

CREATE DISKGROUP

The CREATE DISKGROUP SQL statement is used to create disk groups. When creating a disk group, you specify the following information:

- A unique name to the disk group.
- The redundancy level of the disk group. For Oracle ASM to mirror files, specify the redundancy level as NORMAL REDUNDANCY (2-way mirroring by default for most file types) or HIGH REDUNDANCY (3-way mirroring for all files). Specify EXTERNAL REDUNDANCY if you do not want mirroring by Oracle ASM.
- The disks that are to be formatted as Oracle ASM disks belonging to the disk group.
- Optionally specify the disks as belonging to specific failure groups.
- Optionally specify the type of failure group.
- Optionally specify disk group attributes, such as software compatibility or allocation unit size.

The SQL statement below creates a disk group named data with normal redundancy. It consists of two failure groups: fg1 or fg2 with three disks in each failure group. The data disk group is typically used to store database data files.

```
CREATE DISKGROUP data NORMAL REDUNDANCY
FAILGROUP fg1 DISK
'/devices/diska1' NAME diska1,
'/devices/diska2' NAME diska2,
'/devices/diska3' NAME diska3
FAILGROUP fg2 DISK
'/devices/diskb1' NAME diskb1,
'/devices/diskb2' NAME diskb2,
'/devices/diskb3' NAME diskb3
ATTRIBUTE 'au_size'='2M',
'compatible.asm' = '11.2',
'compatible.rdbms' = '11.2';
```

ALTER DISKGROUP

The ALTER DISKGROUP SQL statement enables you to alter a disk group configuration. It is possible to add, resize, or drop disks while the database remains online. Multiple operations in a single ALTER DISKGROUP statement are both possible and recommended. Grouping operations in a single ALTER DISKGROUP statement can reduce rebalancing operations. Oracle ASM automatically rebalances a disk group when its configuration changes. The V$ASM_OPERATION view allows you to monitor the status of rebalance operations. The following command adds two more disks to the data diskgroup.

```
ALTER DISKGROUP data ADD DISK
'/devices/diska4' NAME diska4,
'/devices/diska5' NAME diska5;
```

When rebalancing a disk group, if the POWER clause is not specified in an ALTER DISKGROUP statement, or if a rebalance is executed implicitly because a disk has been added or dropped, the ASM_POWER_LIMIT initialization parameter determines the power used. The value of this parameter can be adjusted dynamically. Higher power values will cause a rebalance operation to complete faster, but consumes more processing and I/O resources. The default value of 1 minimizes disruption to other applications.

Setup ASM fast mirror resynch

Fast mirror resynch is an Automated Storage Management feature that allows a disk group to restore redundancy quickly after a transient disk failure. When using ASM with disk group redundancy on a version prior to 11g (or with compatibility set lower than 11g), if a disk cannot be accessed, it is taken offline and almost immediately dropped. To restore redundancy, the mirror extent copies are resynchronized in the remaining drives of the disk group. This resynchronization is an extremely costly operation.

When ASM fast mirror resynch is used, if a transient disk failure occurs, the failed drive is automatically taken offline. However, it is not dropped until a predetermined period of time has expired. This time period is set by a new disk group attribute: DISK_REPAIR_TIME. During the time that the drive is offline, ASM tracks modified extents in the disk group. If access to the drive is restored before the drive is dropped, only the modified extents must be resynchronized. Restoring the redundancy is much faster using this process than the 10g model. Fast mirror resynch can only help when the drive failure is transient – a brief power loss, a loose cable, and so forth. If the drive fails such that there is a loss of data or data corruption, fast mirror resynch cannot help.

DISK_REPAIR_TIME

The default value of the DISK_REPAIR_TIME attribute is 3.6 hours. You may change this by issuing the command:

```
ALTER DISKGROUP dgroupMain SET ATTRIBUTE 'disk_repair_time'='5h';
```

Note that if you provide a number for this attribute with no modifier, the default time increment is hours. You can also take drives offline and set the DISK_REPAIR_TIME if performing maintenance. The following example takes disk D2_001 offline and drops it after five minutes.

```
ALTER DISKGROUP dgroupMain OFFLINE DISK D2_001 DROP AFTER 5m;
```

Alternately, you can offline the disk and leave the drop time equal to the DISK_REPAIR_TIME attribute:

```
ALTER DISKGROUP dgroupMain OFFLINE DISK D2_001;
```

You can determine the current setting of the DISK_REPAIR_TIME attribute for the diskgroups in your ASM instance from the V$ASM_ATTRIBUTE view:

```
SELECT group_number, name, value
FROM   v$asm_attribute
WHERE name='disk_repair_time';

GROUP_NUMBER NAME                 VALUE
------------ -------------------- ------------
           1 disk_repair_time     3.6h
           2 disk_repair_time     3.6h
```

Use the mb_backup, md_restore, and repair ASMCMD extensions

The ASM command-line utility (ASMCMD) allows ASM disk identification, disk bad block repair, and backup and restore operations of your ASM environment for faster recovery, among other capabilities. Three of the most important of the ASMCMD commands are md_backup, md_restore, and chkdg.

md_backup

The MD_BACKUP command creates a file containing the metadata for one or more disk groups. The backup file can be used to restore disk groups rapidly in the event of a catastrophic failure of the ASM instance. By default all the mounted disk groups are included in the backup file which is saved in the current working directory. If the name of the backup file is not specified, ASM names the file AMBR_BACKUP_INTERMEDIATE_FILE.

The syntax of the md_backup command is:

```
md_backup [-b location_of_backup] [-g dgname [-g dgname …]]
```

- -b Specifies the location in which you want to store the backup file
- -g Specifies the disk group name to be backed up. Multiple diskgroups can be specified by repeating the –g option.

md_restore

MD_RESTORE is the complement to the MD_BACKUP command. It uses a previously created ASM metadata backup file to recreate diskgroups in an ASM instance. For the test, you particularly want to recognize the options for and differences between the three types of restore.

The syntax of the md_restore command is:

```
md_restore -b backup_file
```

- -b Specifies the backup_file.
- -I Ignore errors. Normally, if md_restore encounters an error, it will stop.
- -t Specifies the type of disk group to be created:
- full - Create disk group and restore metadata
- nodg - Restore metadata only.
- newdg - Create disk group with a different name and restore metadata; -o is required.
- -f Write SQL commands to <sql_script_file> instead of executing them.
- -g Select the disk groups to be restored. If left off, all disk groups will be restored.
- -o Rename disk group old_diskgroup_name to new_diskgroup_name.

chkdg

The ASMCMD chkdg is used to checks the metadata of a disk group and optionally repair it. The syntax of the chkdg command is:

```
chkdg [--repair] diskgroup
```

The following example checks and repairs the dgroupMain disk group.

```
ASMCMD [+] > chkdg --repair dgroupMain
```

Performing User-Managed Backup and Recovery

Recover from a lost TEMP file

If one of more files belonging to the temporary tablespace is lost, any SQL statements that require space in the temporary tablespace will generate an error. If the database is up and you would like to recreate the file immediately, you can do so by creating a new datafile and dropping the old one as follows:

```
SQL> ALTER TABLESPACE temp ADD TEMPFILE
'/u01/app/oracle/oradata/orcl/temp02.dbf' SIZE 50M;
SQL> ALTER TABLESPACE temp DROP TEMPFILE
'/u01/app/oracle/oradata/orcl/temp01.dbf';
```

If the loss or damage to the datafile occurred while the database is down, simply starting the instance will automatically recreate the datafile. If Oracle detects a missing datafile on startup, it will issue the commands to recreate it. You will see a message in the alert log such are:

```
Re-creating tempfile /u01/app/oracle/oradata/orcl/temp01.dbf
```

If the file damage occurred while the database is started, but you would prefer to have the recovery done automatically (and assuming that restarting the database is an option), then shutting down and restarting the instance will recreate the file.

Recover from a lost redo log group

If all members of an online redo log group are damaged, the recovery process depends on the type of online redo log group affected and the whether or not the database is in archivelog mode. If the damaged online redo log group is current and active, then it is needed for crash recovery;

otherwise, it is not. You can determine the status of the group associated with the damage files from V$LOGFILE:

```
SELECT group#, status, member
FROM   v$logfile;

GROUP#     STATUS         MEMBER
-------    -----------    ---------------------
0001                       /oracle/dbs/log1a.f
0001                       /oracle/dbs/log1b.f
0002       INVALID         /oracle/dbs/log2a.f
0002       INVALID         /oracle/dbs/log2b.f
0003                       /oracle/dbs/log3a.f
0003                       /oracle/dbs/log3b.f
```

You can determine which groups are active from the V$LOG view:

```
SELECT group#, status, archived
FROM   v$log;

GROUP#  STATUS      ARCHIVED
------  ---------   -----------
 0001   INACTIVE    YES
 0002   ACTIVE      NO
 0003   CURRENT     NO
```

If all members of an inactive online redo log group are damaged, then the procedure depends on whether it is possible to repair the media problem that damaged the group. If the failure is transient, then fix the problem. The log writer will reuse the redo log group when required. For permanent failures, the damaged redo log group will halt normal database operation when the database tries to use it. The damaged group must be reinitialized manually by issuing the ALTER DATABASE CLEAR LOGFILE statement.

If all members of an active (but not current) log group are damaged and the database is still running, issue the ALTER SYSTEM CHECKPOINT statement. If the checkpoint is successful, then the redo log group will become inactive. At this point you can follow the steps for an inactive online redo log group. If the checkpoint is unsuccessful, or the database has halted, then depending on the archiving mode you must follow the recovery procedures corresponding to the current log group.

The current log group is the one LGWR is currently writing to. If a LGWR I/O operation fails, then LGWR terminates and the instance is terminated. In this case, you must restore a backup, perform incomplete recovery, and open the database with the RESETLOGS option.

Recovering from the Loss of Active Logs in NOARCHIVELOG Mode

If the media failure is temporary, then correct the problem so that the database can reuse the group when required.

- Restore the database from a consistent, whole database backup (data files and control files).
- Mount the database:
- To allow the database to reset the online redo logs, you must first mimic incomplete recovery:

```
RECOVER DATABASE UNTIL CANCEL
CANCEL
```

- Open the database using the RESETLOGS option:

```
ALTER DATABASE OPEN RESETLOGS;
```

- Shut down the database consistently.

```
SHUTDOWN IMMEDIATE
```

- Make a whole database backup.

Recovering from Loss of Active Logs in ARCHIVELOG Mode

- Begin incomplete media recovery, recovering up through the log before the damaged log.
- Ensure that the current name of the lost redo log can be used for a newly created file. If not, then rename the members of the damaged online redo log group to a new location.
- Open the database using the RESETLOGS option:

```
ALTER DATABASE OPEN RESETLOGS;
```

Recover from the loss of password file

If the Oracle password file is lost or damaged, it must be recreated using the orapwd command-line utility. When a new password file is created, orapwd prompts for the SYS password and stores the result in the created password file. The Oracle password file is required to support the administrative privileges SYSDBA and SYSOPER. If this file is lost or damaged, it must be recreated using the orapwd command-line utility. When a new password file is created, orapwd prompts for the SYS password and stores the result in the created password file. The syntax of the ORAPWD command is as follows:

```
ORAPWD FILE=filename [ENTRIES=numusers] [FORCE={Y|N}]
[IGNORECASE={Y|N}]
```

The command arguments of orapwd follow. For all parameters, there are no spaces permitted around the equal sign (=) character.

- **FILE** --Name to assign to the password file. You must supply a complete path. If you supply only a file name, the file is written to the current directory.
- **ENTRIES** -- Maximum number of entries (user accounts) to permit in the file. This is optional.
- **FORCE** -- If Y, permits overwriting an existing password file. This is optional.

- **IGNORECASE** -- If Y, passwords are treated as case-insensitive. This is optional.
- **FORMAT** -- When this argument is set to 12 (the default), ORAPWD creates a database password file in Oracle Database 12c format. The 12c format is required for the file to support SYSBACKUP, SYSDG, and SYSKM administrative privileges. If this argument is set to legacy, then ORAPWD creates a database password file that only supports SYSDBA and SYSOPER privileges.

The following command creates a password file named orapworcl that allows up to 40 privileged users with different passwords.

```
orapwd FILE=orapworcl ENTRIES=40
```

Perform user-managed complete database recovery

Complete database recovery is normally performed when one or more datafiles become damaged or lost. In a complete database recovery, all available redo logs will be applied to recover the database to the current SCN. The following recovery makes these assumptions:

- The current control file is available.
- You have backups of all needed data files.
- All necessary archived redo logs are available.

The basic steps to perform complete recovery while the database is not open follow. You can recover either all damaged data files in one operation or perform individual recovery of each damaged data file in separate operations.

1. If the database is open, query V$RECOVER_FILE to determine which data files must be recovered and why they must be recovered.
2. Query the V$ARCHIVED_LOG and V$RECOVERY_LOG views to determine which archived redo log files are needed.

3. If some archived logs must be restored, restore the required archived redo log files to the location specified by LOG_ARCHIVE_DEST_1.
4. If the database is open, then shut it down.
5. If the files are permanently damaged, then identify the most recent backups for the damaged files. Restore only the data files damaged by the media failure: do not restore undamaged data files or any online redo log files.
6. Use an operating system utility to restore the data files to their default location or to a new location if there is a media failure that cannot be fixed.
7. Connect to the database with administrator privileges. Then start a new instance and mount, but do not open, the database.
8. If you restored one or more damaged data files to alternative locations, then update the control file of the database to reflect the new data file names.
9. Issue a statement to recover the database, tablespace, or data file. For example, enter one of the following RECOVER commands:

```
RECOVER AUTOMATIC DATABASE
RECOVER AUTOMATIC TABLESPACE users
RECOVER AUTOMATIC DATAFILE '?/oradata/trgt/users01.dbf'
```

10. If no archived redo logs are required for complete media recovery, then the database applies all necessary online redo log files and terminates recovery.
11. After recovery terminates, open the database for use

Perform user-managed incomplete database recovery

This section describes steps to perform complete incomplete. When performing an incomplete recovery you must recover all damaged data files in a single operation.

1. If the database is open, query V$RECOVER_FILE to determine which data files must be recovered and why they must be recovered.
2. Query the V$ARCHIVED_LOG and V$RECOVERY_LOG views to determine which archived redo log files are needed.

3. If some archived logs must be restored, restore the required archived redo log files to the location specified by LOG_ARCHIVE_DEST_1.
4. If the database is open, then shut it down.
5. If the files are permanently damaged, then identify the most recent backups for the damaged files. Restore only the data files damaged by the media failure: do not restore undamaged data files or any online redo log files.
6. Use an operating system utility to restore the data files to their default location or to a new location if there is a media failure that cannot be fixed.
7. Connect to the database with administrator privileges. Then start a new instance and mount, but do not open, the database.
8. If you restored one or more damaged data files to alternative locations, then update the control file of the database to reflect the new data file names.
9. Begin cancel-based recovery by issuing the following command in SQL*Plus:

```
RECOVER DATABASE UNTIL CANCEL
```

10. Continue applying redo log files until the last log has been applied to the restored data files, then cancel recovery by executing the following command:

```
CANCEL
```

11. Open the database with the RESETLOGS option. You must always reset the logs after incomplete recovery or recovery with a backup control file.
12. After opening the database with the RESETLOGS option, check the alert log to determine whether the database detected inconsistencies between the data dictionary and the control file.

Perform user-managed and server managed backups

A user-managed backup and recovery strategy is one that does not depend on using Recovery Manager. When performing user-managed backups, a significant number of activities that RMAN performs automatically must instead be performed manually. Before starting the backup, you can use the Oracle data dictionary views to obtain information about the database needed for backup.

Query the V$DATAFILE and V$CONTROLFILE views to identify the data files and control files for your database.

```
SELECT   t.name AS TABLESPACE, f.name AS DATAFILE
FROM     v$tablespace t
         INNER JOIN v$datafile f
         ON t.ts# = f.ts#
ORDER BY t.name;

SELECT name
FROM   v$controlfile;
```

Query the V$BACKUP view to check whether a data file is part of a current online tablespace backup.

```
SELECT t.name AS TB_NAME, d.file# as DF#, d.name AS DF_NAME, b.status
FROM   v$datafile d
       INNER JOIN v$tablespace t
       ON d.ts#=t.ts#
       INNER JOIN v$backup b
       ON b.file#=d.file#
WHERE  b.status='ACTIVE';
```

If the database has been shut down with the NORMAL, IMMEDIATE, or TRANSACTIONAL options, then it is in a consistent state and you can create a usable backup by copying all of the data files with operating system commands. If the database is open, has just had an instance failure or been SHUTDOWN with the ABORT option, the database is in an inconsistent state. Copying the files at this time will create a backup that is inconsistent with the database SCN. Backups taken for a database in NOARCHIVELOG mode must be consistent. When a database is in

ARCHIVELOG mode, it is possible to take inconsistent backups because the archived logs can be used to apply recovery to the datafiles to bring them to a consistent state.

Creating a consistent whole database backup:

1. Shut down the database with the NORMAL, IMMEDIATE, or TRANSACTIONAL options.
2. Use an operating system utility to make backups of all data files, all control files, and the initialization parameter file.
3. Restart the database with the STARTUP command.

Creating an online database backup

Creating a backup of datafiles while the database is active can only be done while the database is in ARCHIVELOG mode. In addition, you must put a read/write tablespace in backup mode when the tablespace is online and the database is open. This is done with the ALTER TABLESPACE ... BEGIN BACKUP statement. When in backup mode, the database copies whole changed data blocks into the redo stream. A backup taken using this method will still require recovery to be performed on it using the archived logs.

1. Set the first tablespace to be backed up into backup mode.
2. Back up the online data files of the tablespace with operating system commands.
3. After backing up the data files of the online tablespace, run the SQL statement ALTER TABLESPACE with the END BACKUP option.
4. Repeat for all tablespaces in the database
5. Archive the unarchived redo logs so that the redo required to recover the tablespace backup is archived.

Creating a server-managed database backup

When using the RMAN utility, all of the steps above can be boiled down to a single command. The RMAN command BACKUP DATABASE is used to perform a whole database backup. I'm pretty sure this test topic was requested by Oracle's marketing department to show how wonderful RMAN is. If you have configured your RMAN defaults correctly, the process to create a server managed database backup is to issue the following command:

```
RMAN> BACKUP DATABASE;
```

Identify the need of backup mode

When performing user-managed backups of the datafiles for an online read-write tablespace while the database is open, it is required that the tablespace first be placed into backup mode. Any time that a tablespace is online and writable, it is possible for the database writer (DBWR) to be updating the file at the same time that the operating system utility is copying it. When this happens, it is possible for the utility to read a block while it is in a partially-updated state. In this case, the block that is copied to the backup media would contain some newer data and some older data. This type of logical corruption is known as a fractured block. Fractured blocks are not consistent with any SCN and Oracle does not normally store sufficient information to repair them.

This situation can be resolved by placing datafiles into backup mode with the ALTER DATABASE or ALTER TABLESPACE statement with the BEGIN BACKUP clause. Once a tablespace has been put into backup mode, Oracle writes the before image for an entire block to the redo stream before making changes to it. The changes made to the block are also stored in the online redo log. Backup mode also freezes the data file checkpoint until the file is removed from backup mode. During recovery, the before image can be used to repair fractured blocks.

RMAN itself does not require extra logging or backup mode because it knows the format of data blocks and will never back up fractured blocks. RMAN also does not need to freeze the data file header checkpoint. It is aware of the order in which the blocks are read, so it can always capture a known good checkpoint.

Back up and recover a control file

The control file is critical to recovery of an Oracle database and so backing it up is of paramount importance. There are numerous ways to back up the control file. If you are using RMAN as your backup tool, the easiest of these is simply to configure RMAN to automatically back up the control file and server parameter file whenever a backup record is added. The autobackup feature is enabled and disabled as follows:

```
CONFIGURE CONTROLFILE AUTOBACKUP ON;
```

Even if CONTROLFILE AUTOBACKUP is not enabled, performing a whole database backup in RMAN will include a copy of the control file. The RMAN command BACKUP DATABASE is used to perform a whole database backup.

```
BACKUP DATABASE;
```

Outside of RMAN, there are two ALTER DATABASE commands that can be used to back up a control file. You can back up the control file to a binary file using the following statement:

```
ALTER DATABASE BACKUP CONTROLFILE TO '/oracle/backup/control.bkp';
```

Alternately, the following command writes a SQL script to a trace file that can be used to reproduce the control file. The alert log will contain the name and location of the trace file.

```
ALTER DATABASE BACKUP CONTROLFILE TO TRACE;
```

Finally, for a user managed backup while the database is shut down, you can use operating system commands to copy the control file.

Recovering the Database with a Backup Control File

In a recovery scenario where all copies of the current control file are lost or damaged, then you must restore and mount a backup control file. Copy the backup control file to all of the locations listed in the CONTROL_FILES initialization parameter. After the files are in place, the RECOVER command must be issued, even if no datafiles have been restored.

```
RECOVER DATABASE USING BACKUP CONTROLFILE UNTIL CANCEL;
```

Once the restore operation has been completed, open the database with the RESETLOGS option.

Database Administration

Installing and Upgrading

Install Oracle Database 11g

There are a number of operating system environment variables that are utilized by Oracle and the Oracle Universal Installer. The OS environment must be properly set prior to running the installer in order for the installation to function correctly. OUI is normally run from the oracle account of the operating system. You must configure the environment of the oracle user prior to initiating the install. Some environment variables must be set, and others are optional, but setting them prior to the install can avoid difficulties later. You should view the appropriate installation guide for the operating system under which you will be performing the install for details on setting environment variables.

Under Linux, the following environment variables must be set:

- The default file mode creation mask (umask) must be set to 022
- The XWindows DISPLAY variable must be set properly.
- The TMP and TMPDIR environment variables must be pointing to the tmp mount point.

The following Oracle environment variables don't have to be set, but ideally should be.

- ORACLE_BASE – sets the base of the directory structure use for OFA.
- ORACLE_SID – Sets the initial instance name used by the OS account.
- ORACLE_HOME – Specifies the directory where the Oracle software is installed.
- NLS_LANG – Specifies language, territory and character set settings.
- LD_LIBRARY_PATH – Specifies the path to Oracle-installed libraries for Linux.

Running the Oracle Universal Installer

For any type of installation process, start Oracle Universal Installer and install the software, as follows:

1. Log in as the OS user that will be the software owner (typically, oracle).
2. Mount the disk containing the installation media if required.
3. To start Oracle Universal Installer, issue the command /directory_path/runInstaller, where directory_path is the path of the database directory on the installation media.
4. Select the product to be installed.
5. Select either the basic or advanced installation.
6. Follow the prompts in the install screens.

If you chose to create a starter database during the installation, OUI will invoke the Oracle Net Configuration Assistant and the Oracle Database Configuration Assistant (DBCA). The Net Configuration Assistance will walk you through the steps to configure the Oracle Listener and naming methods. DBCA is the application that will actually create the starter database.

DBCA

Oracle's Database Configuration Assistant (DBCA) is a much more automated means of creating a database than using the CREATE DATABASE statement. In addition, once DBCA has completed, the database is immediately ready to use. It's possible for DBCA to be launched by OUI, depending upon the type of install used. DBCA can also be launched as a standalone tool at any point after the Oracle software has been installed.

DBCA has two modes of operation: interactive mode or noninteractive/silent mode. The interactive mode makes use of a graphical user interface and guides you through creating and configuring a database. The noninteractive mode allows you to create the database via a script. DBCA is run in noninteractive mode by specifying command-line arguments, a response file, or both. To start DBCA:

Log on to your computer as a member of the group that is authorized to install Oracle and to create and run the database. To start DBCA on UNIX or Linux, or at the command-line prompt in Microsoft Windows, enter the following command: dbca. The dbca executable is located in the ORACLE_HOME/bin directory. Once started, the DBCA user interface guides you through a step-by-step process to create a database.

Creating a Database Using DBCA

- **Operations** – Select Create a Database and click Next to start the guided workflow for creating a database.
- **Database Templates** – Preconfigured or user-created templates allow you to select the type of database to create, with settings optimized for a particular style of workload.
- **Database Identification** – Enter the Global Database Name and the system identifier.
- **Management Options** – Allows you to set up your database so it can be managed with Oracle Enterprise Manager.
- **Database Credentials** – You will specify the passwords for the database administrative accounts.
- **Database File Locations** – You will specify the type of storage and the locations for the Oracle database files. The files might be stored as operating system files, ASM files, or on a Clustered File System.
- **Recovery Configuration** – You will define recovery options such as a fast recovery area and archivelog mode for your database.
- **Database Content** – The database can be created with content using either the sample schemas or custom scripts.
- **Initialization Parameters** – This screen allows you to access windows to change the default initialization parameter settings.
- **Database Storage** – Allows you to verify and/or change the database storage structure.
- **Creation Options** – Allows you create the database, save the settings as a template, or generate database creation scripts.

Creating a Database with Noninteractive/Silent DBCA

The following example creates a database by passing command-line arguments to DBCA:

```
dbca -silent -createDatabase -templateName General_Purpose.dbc -
gdbname oraprod -sid oraprod -responseFile NO_VALUE -characterSet
AL32UTF8 -memoryPercentage 30 -emConfiguration LOCAL
Enter SYSTEM user password:
password
Enter SYS user password:
password
Copying database files
1% complete
3% complete
...
```

It's possible to have a completely silent operation by redirecting **stdout** to a file. However, to do this you must supply passwords for the administrative accounts in command-line arguments or in a response file. You can view all of the DBCA command-line arguments, by running dbca with the parameter -help (dbca -help).

Deleting a Database with DBCA

To delete a database in DBCA, you will execute dbca from a terminal window and click through past the welcome screen. From the Operations screen you can select 'Delete a Database.' You will be given a list of databases. Select the database to be deleted. Click finish and then confirm the deletion when asked by DBCA.

Upgrade your database to Oracle Database 11g

When performing a manual upgrade to Oracle 11g, there are five scripts that must be run for the upgrade process to complete successfully. It's important that you remember function of each and the order in which they get run. When upgrading a database, the very <u>first</u> step is to make sure that you have a good backup. After taking a backup, you'll shut the database down and issue the command "startup upgrade" to open the database in upgrade mode. Upgrade mode disables system triggers and prepares the data dictionary for update.

Once the database is started in upgrade mode, you can begin running the scripts.

1. **utlu111i.sql** -- This is the Pre-Upgrade information tool. This script is technically a precursor to the upgrade. It generates a report that contains required and recommended changes to make to the database before beginning the upgrade process. It might be necessary to increase the size of SYSAUX, change or remove parameters, among other actions. Once the information tool indicates the database is ready, the upgrade can be performed.
2. **catupgrd.sql** -- This is the script that will make the actual changes to the database structure to bring it to the 11g model. If the script is stopped or fails before completion, it can be re-run multiple times. At completion, the catupgrd.sql script will shut the database down. Once it has completed, the database should be restarted in normal mode.
3. **utlu111s.sql** – This is the post upgrade status script and should be executed once catupgrd.sql has completed successfully. This script verifies that all components have been upgraded to 11g. If some have not, you will need to run the catupgrd.sql script again. Note that the Pre-Upgrade and Post-Upgrade scripts have very similar names. You need to remember which is which for the test.
4. **catuppst.sql** -- This is the Post upgrade actions script. Once the status script shows all components have been upgraded to 11g, this script must be executed. The catuppst.sql script is new with 11g and performs numerous upgrade tasks that don't require the database to be in upgrade mode.
5. **utlrp.sql** -- This script recompiles and revalidates any database objects shown as INVALID in the Post-Upgrade Status script. It can be executed simultaneously with catuppst.sql (or before or after).

While it's not explicitly listed as a test component, I'll note that the script **catdwgrd.sql** is what you would use if you wanted to downgrade your database back to the pre-upgrade version.

Database Upgrade Assistant (DBUA)

It's also possible (and in most cases preferable) to upgrade to Oracle 11g using the Database Upgrade Assistant or DBUA. There's much less to remember (and much less to be tested on) with DBUA. You should know that DBUA can upgrade database and ASM instances simultaneously, whereas manual upgrades must upgrade them separately. DBUA is also somewhat faster at the end as it can recompile objects in parallel on multi-CPU systems.

The following enhancements have been added to DBUA:

- For single-instance databases, Oracle DBUA configuration utility enables you to upgrade from Oracle Database XE to Oracle Database 11g.
- You can move datafiles to ASM, OFS, or other storage devices, such as Storage Area Networks (SAN) and Network Area Storage (NAS), as part of the upgrade.
- The directory that you specify when you are prompted for ORACLE_BASE by Oracle Universal Installer is stored in the Oracle home inventory. DBUA uses this value to derive the default database locations and the DIAGNOSTIC_DEST parameter.
- The command line option AUTOEXTEND facilitates auto extending of the data files as a part of the upgrade. This option autoextends the data files during the upgrade and turns the autoextend back to its original settings after the upgrade.

Oracle Direct NFS

Starting with Oracle 11g, a native NFS client capability was imbedded as part of the Oracle Database kernel. This feature improves performance and manageability when using Network File System drives. The Direct NFS Client improves I/O performance by incorporating Oracle-specific optimizations and eliminating the overhead from the operating system kernel NFS support. In addition, Direct NFS simplifies configuration by eliminating the need to manually tune most of the NFS parameters.

To use Direct NFS, the NFS file systems must first be mounted and available via the operating system kernel. Direct NFS does *not* mount the drives. The specific mount options used by the operating system aren't important, as Direct NFS Client manages Oracle's access to the drive. The Direct NFS Client will use either a new configuration file called 'oranfstab' or the mount tab file (/etc/mtab on Linux) to determine the mount point settings for NFS storage devices. Oracle first looks for the mount settings in $ORACLE_HOME/dbs/oranfstab, which would specify the Direct NFS Client settings for a single database. Second, Oracle looks for settings in /etc/oranfstab, which specifies the NFS mounts available to all Oracle databases on that host. Finally, Oracle reads the mount tab file (/etc/mtab on Linux) to identify available NFS mounts. If duplicate entries exist in the configuration files, Direct NFS Client will use the first entry found. In addition to populating one of these files with the NFS mount settings, you must replace the standard Oracle Disk Manager (ODM) library with one that supports Direct NFS Client. A sample oranfstab file would look similar to the following:

```
server: MyNFSServer1
path: 192.168.1.1
path: 192.168.1.2
path: 192.168.1.3
path: 192.168.1.4
export: /vol/oradata1 mount: /mnt/oradata1
```

Once the file exists, the following commands will enable the Direct NFS Client ODM Library

```
$ cd $ORACLE_HOME/lib
$ cp libodm11.so libodm11.so_stub
$ ln -s libnfsodm11.so libodm11.so
```

Use online patching

Prior to Release 11g, all Oracle patches contained .o (object) files and/or .a (archive) libraries. Installing them required a relink of the RDBMS binary and therefore meant the database had to be shut down before the patch could be applied. With 11g, some patches are available as online patches. These contain .so files, which are dynamic/shared libraries, and they do not require a relink of the RDBMS binary. Because a relink is not needed, online patches can be applied or rolled back while the database instance is running. This simplifies administration, because no downtime is needed. It also means that installing or de-installing Online Patches is faster -- potentially taking just a few seconds. Online patches will be installed using the opatch utility.

The benefits of online patches include the following:

- No downtime is required
- They persist across shutdowns
- They allow rolling patches in RAC
- They have a fast installation

There are few downsides to online patches:

- They require more memory
- Online patching isn't available on all platforms
- Not all patches are available as hot patches

Memory Management

Implement Automatic Memory Management

Once upon a time, tuning the various memory pools of an Oracle server was a very manual process and one that involved a fair amount of guesswork. Over the past several releases, Oracle has adding increasing amounts of automation to this process. With 11g, a single parameter allows the Database instance to automatically manage all of the memory pools. When the MEMORY_TARGET parameter is to a target memory size, the Oracle instance will grab this much memory on startup and allocate it automatically to the various memory pools.

Optionally you can specify a maximum memory size with the MEMORY_MAX_TARGET initialization parameter. The MEMORY_TARGET initialization parameter is dynamic and can be changed without restarting the database. The MEMORY_MAX_TARGET is not dynamic and requires a shutdown to change. It serves as an upper limit on the value assigned to the MEMORY_TARGET parameter so that you cannot accidentally set it too high.

When using Automatic memory management, the instance distributes memory between the SGA and PGA automatically. The instance dynamically redistributes memory between the two as memory requirements change. Databases created with DBCA using the basic installation option will have automatic memory management enabled by default. If a database is not currently using Automatic Memory Management, you can enable it using the following commands:

```
ALTER SYSTEM SET MEMORY_TARGET = nM;
ALTER SYSTEM SET SGA_TARGET = 0;
ALTER SYSTEM SET PGA_AGGREGATE_TARGET = 0;
```

Optionally you can issue the following command:

```
ALTER SYSTEM SET MEMORY_MAX_TARGET = nM SCOPE = SPFILE;
```

The relationships between the four parameters utilized by Automatic Memory Management are:

- **memory_target** – When MEMORY_TARGET is set, the database will allocate this much memory on startup, by default granting 60% to the SGA and 40% to the PGA. Over time, as the database runs, it will redistribute memory as needed between the system global area (SGA) and the instance program global area (instance PGA). If MEMORY_TARGET is not set, automatic memory management is not enabled, even if you have set a value for MEMORY_MAX_TARGET.
- **memory_max_target** – When set, this determines the maximum amount of memory that Oracle will grab from the OS for the SGA and PGA. If this value is not set, it will default to the MEMORY_TARGET value.
- **sga_target** – This value is not required if using automatic memory management. If this value is set and MEMORY_TARGET is also set, then the value of SGA_TARGET becomes the minimum amount of memory allocated to the SGA by automatic memory management.
- **pga_aggregate_target** – This value is not required if using automatic memory management. If this value is set and MEMORY_TARGET is also set, then the value of PGA_AGGREGATE_TARGET becomes the minimum amount of memory allocated to the PGA by automatic memory management.

Manually configure SGA parameters

Automatic Shared Memory Management (ASMM) was the precursor to Automatic Memory Management (AMM). If you want to use ASMM instead of AMM, the total amount of SGA memory available to an instance is specified using the SGA_TARGET initialization parameter. Oracle will automatically distribute this memory among the various SGA components. When using ASMM, a few components of the SGA are still manually sized, including:

- **LOG_BUFFER** -- The log buffer.
- **DB_KEEP_CACHE_SIZE** -- The keep buffer cache.
- **DB_RECYCLE_CACHE_SIZE** -- The recycle buffer cache.
- **DB_nK_CACHE_SIZE** -- Nonstandard block size buffer caches

Any memory allocated to the manually-sized components is subtracted from the SGA_TARGET value and the remainder is allocated among the automatically Sized SGA Components:

- **SHARED_POOL_SIZE** -- The shared pool.
- **LARGE_POOL_SIZE** -- The large pool
- **JAVA_POOL_SIZE** -- The Java pool
- **DB_CACHE_SIZE** -- The buffer cache
- **STREAMS_POOL_SIZE** -- The Streams pool

Configure automatic PGA memory management

Oracle will automatically manage the amount of memory allocated to the instance PGA by default. The initialization parameter PGA_AGGREGATE_TARGET can be utilized to explicitly control this value. When set, the database will attempt to keep the total amount of PGA memory allocated below this target. When creating a database using the DBCA utility, it is possible to specify a value for the total instance PGA. If a value is specified, DBCA will use this value in the the PGA_AGGREGATE_TARGET initialization parameter in the server parameter file. When a value is not specified, DBCA will use a reasonable default. When a database is created using the CREATE DATABASE SQL statement and a text initialization parameter file, it is possible to provide a value for PGA_AGGREGATE_TARGET. If the parameter is omitted, the database will choose a default value.

The following dynamic performance views provide statistics on allocation and use of work area memory:

- V$SYSSTAT
- V$SESSTAT
- V$PGASTAT
- V$SQL_WORKAREA
- V$SQL_WORKAREA_ACTIVE

The V$PROCESS view contains three columns that report the PGA memory allocated and used by an Oracle Database process:

- PGA_USED_MEM
- PGA_ALLOCATED_MEM
- PGA_MAX_MEM

Storage Management

Create and maintain bigfile tablespaces

Standard tablespaces in Oracle consists of one or more operating system files. By contrast, a bigfile tablespace consists of a single (potentially very large) file. Bigfile tablespaces provide a number of advantages over smallfile tablespaces:

- The datafile for a bigfile tablespace can be huge. A bigfile tablespace with a 32K blocks can have a 128 terabyte datafile. They allow Oracle to hold more data with fewer datafiles. Because the total number of datafiles an Oracle database can have is limited, it also increases the maximum storage capacity of the database.
- Fewer datafiles allows for a lower setting for DB_FILES initialization parameter, which reduces the amount of SGA space required for datafile information.
- The MAXDATAFILES parameter of the CREATE DATABASE and CREATE CONTROLFILE statements can be lowered to reduce the size of the control file.
- Bigfile tablespaces provide datafile transparency. The ALTER TABLESPACE statement allows you perform operations on tablespaces, rather than the underlying individual datafiles.

Bigfile tablespaces are supported only for locally managed tablespaces with automatic segment space management. Undo, temporary, and SYSTEM tablespaces cannot be created using the bigfile option. Bigfile tablespaces should be created on a filesystem controlled by a volume manager that supports striping or RAID.

Bigfile tablespaces are created when the BIGFILE keyword is specified in the CREATE TABLESPACE statement. Oracle will automatically create a locally managed tablespace with automatic segment space management. If the CREATE TABLESPACE statement explicitly specifies EXTENT MANAGEMENT DICTIONARY or SEGMENT SPACE MANAGEMENT

MANUAL, an error will be returned. The remaining syntax of the statement is the same as for the CREATE TABLESPACE statement.

```
CREATE BIGFILE TABLESPACE bf_tbs
DATAFILE '/u02/oracle/data/bftbs01.dbf' SIZE 50G
...
```

The following views contain a BIGFILE column that identifies a tablespace as a bigfile tablespace:

- DBA_TABLESPACES
- USER_TABLESPACES
- V$TABLESPACE

Rename tablespaces

The ALTER TABLESPACE statement can be used to rename a permanent or temporary tablespace if required. When a tablespace is renamed, Oracle updates all references to the tablespace name in the data dictionary, control file, and all online datafile headers. he tablespace ID remains the same. Any users who had the tablespace as their default will continue to do so after the rename operation. Some restrictions to the operation include:

- The COMPATIBLE parameter must be 10.0.0 or higher.
- The SYSTEM and SYSAUX tablespaces cannot be renamed.
- The tablespace and all datafiles must be online.
- If the tablespace is read only, its datafile headers are not updated. A message will be written to the alert log indicating that datafile headers have not been renamed. The data dictionary and control file are updated.

Renaming an undo tablespace has some additional considerations.

- If a server parameter file was used to start the instance and the tablespace name is specified as the UNDO_TABLESPACE for any instance, the tablespace name is changed to the new tablespace name in the server parameter file.
- If the instance was started using a traditional initialization parameter file, a message will be written to the alert log stating that the initialization parameter file must be manually changed.

The syntax for renaming a tablespace is:

```
ALTER TABLESPACE users RENAME TO users_new;
```

Create a default permanent tablespace

It is possible to set a default permanent tablespace to be used for user accounts that have not been explicitly assigned a default tablespace. This feature was added to prevent the nasty alternative, which was newly-created users having their default permanent tablespace become SYSTEM when one was not assigned. Both the CREATE DATABASE and ALTER DATABASE statements have a DEFAULT TABLESPACE clause. The following example sets the default permanent tablespace to USERS:

```
ALTER DATABASE DEFAULT TABLESPACE users;
```

The current settings for the default tablespaces can be determined by querying the database_properties view:

```
SELECT property_name, property_value
FROM   database_properties
WHERE  property_name like '%TABLESPACE';

PROPERTY_NAME                  PROPERTY_VALUE
------------------------------ --------------
DEFAULT_TEMP_TABLESPACE        TEMP2
DEFAULT_PERMANENT_TABLESPACE   USERS
```

When a default permanent tablespace is set (or changed) all objects created by users who do not have a default tablespace explicitly assigned will be created there unless the create statement explicitly references another tablespace.

Space Management

Manage resumable space allocation

Resumable space allocation allows for large database operations to be suspended and later resumed in the event of a space allocation failure. Prior to this feature, when such an operation ran out of space, it immediately failed and was rolled back. Even with the new capability, a statement executes in a resumable mode only if its session has been enabled for resumable space allocation.

If a resumable statement is suspended, the error causing the suspension is reported in the alert log, and the system issues the Resumable Session Suspended alert. If the user has a trigger on the AFTER SUSPEND system event, it will be executed. If the error condition is resolved before the timeout period expires, the suspended statement resumes automatically and the Resumable Session Suspended alert is cleared. If a statement is suspended for the full timeout interval (the default is two hours), it will wake up and return the exception to the user. It is possible for a resumable statement to be suspended and resumed multiple times during execution.

There are three classes of correctable errors:

- Out of space
- Maximum extents reached
- Space quota exceeded

Enabling and Disabling Resumable Space Allocation

Resumable space allocation is only possible if the session a statement is executed in has resumable mode enabled. Resumable mode can be enabled at the system level with the RESUMABLE_TIMEOUT initialization parameter, or users can enable it at the session level using the ALTER SESSION statement. Users can only do this if they have been granted the RESUMABLE system privilege.

By default, the RESUMABLE_TIMEOUT parameter is set to 0. This disables resumable for all sessions by default. Providing a non-zero value will enable resumable space allocation by default for all sessions with the supplied number of seconds. The parameter can be changed dynamically by issuing an ALTER SYSTEM SET RESUMABLE_TIMEOUT command with the desired value. Within a session, a user can alter the resumable behavior with the ALTER SESSION SET RESUMABLE_TIMEOUT statement.

A user can enable or disable resumable mode for a session with ALTER SESSION:

```
ALTER SESSION ENABLE RESUMABLE;
ALTER SESSION DISABLE RESUMABLE;
```

When resumable mode is enabled for a session, the following statement specifies that resumable transactions will time out and error after 3600 seconds:

```
ALTER SESSION ENABLE RESUMABLE TIMEOUT 3600;
```

When enabling resumable statements, it is possible to give them a name. If a name is not set, a statement name will default to 'User username(userid), Session sessionid, Instance instanceid'.

```
ALTER SESSION ENABLE RESUMABLE TIMEOUT 3600 NAME 'Really Huge Table
Insert';
```

The following views can be queried to obtain information about the status of resumable statements:

- **DBA_RESUMABLE & USER_RESUMABLE** -- Contain rows for all currently executing or suspended resumable statements. They can be used to monitor the progress of, or obtain specific information about, resumable statements.
- **V$SESSION_WAIT** -- When a statement is suspended the session invoking the statement is put into a wait state. A row is inserted

into this view for the session with the EVENT column containing "statement suspended, wait error to be cleared".

The DBMS_RESUMABLE package helps control resumable space allocation. The following procedures can be invoked:

- **ABORT(sessionID)** -- This procedure aborts a suspended resumable statement.
- **GET_SESSION_TIMEOUT(sessionID)** -- This function returns the current timeout value of resumable space allocation for the session with sessionID.
- **SET_SESSION_TIMEOUT(sessionID, timeout)** -- This procedure sets the timeout interval of resumable space allocation for the session with sessionID.
- **GET_TIMEOUT()** -- This function returns the current timeout value of resumable space allocation for the current session.
- **SET_TIMEOUT(timeout)** -- This procedure sets a timeout value for resumable space allocation for the current session.

Reclaim wasted space from tables and indexes by using the segment shrink functionality

The online segment shrink capability of Oracle allows you to reclaim fragmented free space below the high watermark in a segment. Shrinking a segment provides the following benefits:

- Compaction of data leads to better cache utilization.
- Compacted data requires fewer blocks to be scanned in full table scans.

Segment shrink is an online, in-place operation that does not interfere with DML operations or queries. Concurrent DML operations are blocked for a short time at the end of the shrink operation, when the space is deallocated. Indexes are maintained during the shrink operation and remain usable after completion. No extra disk space needs to be allocated. Segment shrink reclaims unused space both above and below the high water mark. By default, a shrink operation compacts the segment, adjusts the high water mark, and releases the reclaimed space.

Segment shrink requires that rows be moved to new locations. You must first enable row movement in the object and disable any rowid-based triggers. Shrink operations can be performed only on segments in locally managed tablespaces with automatic segment space management (ASSM). Within an ASSM tablespace, all segment types are eligible for online segment shrink except the following:

- IOT mapping tables
- Tables with rowid based materialized views
- Tables with function-based indexes
- SECUREFILE LOBs
- Compressed tables

Invoking Online Segment Shrink

You can shrink space in a table, index-organized table, index, partition, subpartition, materialized view, or materialized view log. You do this using ALTER TABLE, ALTER INDEX, ALTER MATERIALIZED VIEW, or ALTER MATERIALIZED VIEW LOG statement with the SHRINK SPACE clause. There are two optional clauses that control the behavior of the shrink operation:

- **COMPACT** – This clause divides the shrink segment operation into two phases. When specified, the Database defragments the segment space and compacts the table rows but does not reset the high water mark or deallocate space. You can reissue the SHRINK SPACE clause without the COMPACT clause during off-peak hours to complete the shrink operation.
- **CASCADE** – This clause extends the segment shrink operation to all dependent segments of the object.

Examples

Shrink a table and all of its dependent segments:

```
ALTER TABLE employees SHRINK SPACE CASCADE;
```

Shrink a single partition of a partitioned table:

```
ALTER TABLE customers MODIFY PARTITION cust_P1 SHRINK SPACE;
```

Rebuild indexes online

During an index rebuild, an existing index is used as the data source to build a duplicate. Index rebuilds allow administrators to change storage characteristics or move in index to a new tablespace. During the rebuild, any intra-block fragmentation will be eliminated. The operation will create a new tree, shrinking the height if applicable. An index rebuild operation has better performance when compared to dropping the index and using the CREATE INDEX statement to re-create it.

The following statement rebuilds the existing index ocp_emps:

```
ALTER INDEX ocp_emps REBUILD;
```

It is also possible to rebuild the index online. Rebuilding online allows the base tables to be updated concurrent with the rebuild operation. The following statement rebuilds the ocp_emps index online:

```
ALTER INDEX ocp_emps REBUILD ONLINE;
```

Reduce space related error conditions through proactively managing tablespace usage

A tablespace that is locally managed uses bitmaps within the tablespace itself to track all extent information. Local management has several benefits over traditional tablespaces where this information is stored in the data dictionary:

- Space allocations and deallocations modify locally managed resources. This makes them fast and concurrent, resulting in enhanced performance.
- Locally managed temporary tablespaces do not generate any undo or redo.
- If the AUTOALLOCATE clause is specified, the database automatically selects the appropriate extent size.
- Reliance on the data dictionary is reduced, reducing contention in times of high activity to tables.
- There is no need to coalesce free extents.

Any tablespace can be locally managed, including SYSTEM and SYSAUX. There are maintenance procedures in the DBMS_SPACE_ADMIN package specific to locally managed tablespaces.

The syntax to create a locally managed tablespace, is the keyword LOCAL in the EXTENT MANAGEMENT clause of the CREATE TABLESPACE statement. The default value for new permanent tablespaces is 'EXTENT MANAGEMENT LOCAL AUTOALLOCATE'. Specifying this clause is optional unless you do not want local management or you want to use the UNIFORM keyword rather than AUTOALLOCATE. When the AUTOALLOCATE keyword is used, the database will manage extents automatically. If you want the tablespace to utilize uniform extents of a specific size, you must specify the UNIFORM keyword. The two commands below will have identical effects:

```
CREATE TABLESPACE ocpts DATAFILE '/u02/oracle/data/ocpts01.dbf' SIZE
50M
EXTENT MANAGEMENT LOCAL AUTOALLOCATE;

CREATE TABLESPACE ocpts DATAFILE '/u02/oracle/data/ocpts01.dbf' SIZE
50M;
```

There are two methods that Oracle Database can use to manage segment space in a locally managed tablespace. Manual space management uses freelists to manage free space in a segment. Automatic segment space management uses bitmaps. Automatic segment space management is more efficient and is the default for all new permanent, locally managed tablespaces. You can explicitly enable it with the SEGMENT SPACE MANAGEMENT AUTO clause:

```
CREATE TABLESPACE ocpts DATAFILE '/u02/oracle/data/ocpts01.dbf' SIZE
50M
EXTENT MANAGEMENT LOCAL AUTOALLOCATE
SEGMENT SPACE MANAGEMENT AUTO;
```

Compression

When you create a tablespace, it's possible to specify that all tables created in it be compressed by default. This is done with the DEFAULT keyword, followed by the compression type to be used. There are four different compression options:

- **DEFAULT COMPRESS [BASIC]** – Basic table compression compresses data inserted by direct path load only and supports limited data types and SQL operations.
- **DEFAULT COMPRESS FOR OLTP** – All tables created in the tablespace will use OLTP compression, unless otherwise specified. OLTP table compression is intended for OLTP applications and compresses data manipulated by any SQL operation.
- **DEFAULT COMPRESS FOR QUERY [LOW|HIGH]** – This compression method can result in high CPU overhead and works best for direct-path load. Rows inserted without using direct-path insert and updated rows go to a block with a less compressed format and have lower compression level.

- **DEFAULT COMPRESS FOR ARCHIVE [LOW|HIGH]** – This compression method can result in high CPU overhead and works best for direct-path load. Rows inserted without using direct-path insert and updated rows go to a block with a less compressed format and have lower compression level.

You can get more information on the compression types from the Oracle Database Administrator's Guide. Tables created in a tablespace with the compression option enabled will default to that method. However, you can create tables uncompressed or using a different method by supplying a compression clause in the CREATE TABLE statement. If you alter the default compression in a tablespace, all new tables created will default to the new method, but existing tables are unchanged.

Use different storage options to improve the performance of queries

SQL Queries access the data stored in tables (obviously). However, the type of queries that will be executed against a table, its eventual size, and its relationship to other tables in the database all have query performance implications. Administrators should consider these when making decisions about the storage options used when creating a table. There are four broad classes of table storage types: Heap organized, Index organized, Clustered, and Partitioned.

Heap-organized tables are the general-purpose tables that make up the majority of table objects created in Oracle databases. Data in these tables is stored in an unorganized fashion. Unless there is a specific reason for using another type of table, data should be stored in heap-organized tables.

Index-organized tables (IOTs) store data in a B-tree index structure sorted by the primary key of the table. The index entries of the B-tree store not only the key columns but all of the nonkey columns of the table as well. Storing the table data in this fashion provides fast random access on the primary key because an index-only scan is sufficient to locate the data. IOTs also provide fast range access on queries that use the primary key.

A clustered table is any table that is part of a cluster. A cluster is created using a group of tables that share common columns and are often used together. When organized as a cluster, these tables will share data blocks for the common columns (known as the cluster key). Storing the related rows of multiple tables together in this fashion provides two primary benefits:

- Disk I/O is reduced and access time improves for joins of clustered tables.
- The cluster key value is stored only once each in the cluster and the cluster index, no matter how many rows of different tables contain the value.

Partitioned tables allow administrators to break the data stored in the table into pieces. These pieces are called partitions or subpartitions. Each partition of a table is separate data dictionary object. Each partition of a single table can have different settings for physical attributes such as compression, storage settings, and tablespace. This allows administrators to fine-tune the physical structure of a table for availability and performance.

The previous section discussed four compression options that can be set as the tablespace default: BASIC, OLTP, COMPRESS FOR QUERY, and COMPRESS FOR ARCHIVE. No matter what the tablespace default is, administrators can chose to create individual tables (or individual partitions) using any of the options (or no compression at all). Compressing data in a table not only saves disk space, it also reduces memory use in the database buffer cache. It can also improve query execution performance during reads. There is a CPU cost for tables using compression during data loading and DML operations. However, the reduced I/O requirements of reading the data back (more rows per block) can make up for this cost.

Use automatic undo retention tuning and temporary tuning

Any time that automatic undo management is enabled, there is an undo retention period. This is the minimum amount of time that the database will try to keep old undo information from being overwritten. The undo retention period is based on the undo tablespace size and system activity. It is possible to use the UNDO_RETENTION initialization parameter to specify a minimum undo retention period.

It the undo tablespace is fixed size, the value of UNDO_RETENTION is ignored. The database automatically uses system activity and undo tablespace size to tune the undo retention period for the best possible retention. For an undo tablespace set to AUTOEXTEND, the database will attempt to honor the specified UNDO_RETENTION period. When space is low, the tablespace will auto-extend (up to the MAXSIZE) instead of overwriting unexpired undo information. If the MAXSIZE is reached, the database may not be able to meet the UNDO_RETENTION value. The minimum undo retention period (in seconds) can be set in two ways:

- Set UNDO_RETENTION in the initialization parameter file.

  ```
  UNDO_RETENTION = 2000
  ```

- The UNDO_RETENTION value can be modified dynamically using the ALTER SYSTEM statement.

  ```
  ALTER SYSTEM SET UNDO_RETENTION = 3000;
  ```

The effect of an UNDO_RETENTION parameter change can only be honored if the current undo tablespace has sufficient space.

When using a fixed-size undo tablespace, the Undo Advisor is valuable for estimating the optimum size. It can be accessed through Oracle Enterprise Manager Express or through DBMS_ADVISOR. The Undo Advisor uses AWR data to create its analysis, so there must be sufficient workload statistics available for it to make accurate recommendations. When using the Undo Advisor, two values must be estimated:

- The length of the expected longest running query.
- The longest interval required for Oracle Flashback operations

The larger of these two values is used as input to the Undo Advisor. The Undo Advisor does not alter the size of the undo tablespace, it only offers a recommended size. You must use ALTER DATABASE statements to change the tablespace data file size. The following example changes an undo tablespace with a file called undotbs.dbf to a fixed size of 400MB.

```
ALTER DATABASE DATAFILE '/u01/oracle/dbs/undotbs.dbf' RESIZE 400M;
ALTER DATABASE DATAFILE '/u01/oracle/dbs/undotbs.dbf' AUTOEXTEND OFF;
```

The RETENTION_GUARANTEE clause is used to guarantee the success of long-running queries or Oracle Flashback operations. When enabled, the specified minimum undo retention is guaranteed. Oracle will never overwrite unexpired undo data even when doing so means that transactions fail from lack of space in the undo tablespace. When retention guarantee is disabled (the default), the database can overwrite unexpired undo when space is low. The RETENTION GUARANTEE clause can be specified for an undo tablespace at create time with either the CREATE DATABASE or CREATE UNDO TABLESPACE statement. The clause can be used to modify an existing tablespace using the ALTER TABLESPACE statement. Retention guarantee is disabled with the RETENTION NOGUARANTEE clause.

Temporary Undo

Any time a transaction is performed in the Oracle database, it is necessary for Oracle to create undo information about the transaction in order to maintain transaction consistency. This is true event for data written to temporary tables. While the data written to the temporary tables generates no redo (because there is no need to recover them). However, the undo data generated by operations on temporary tables is written to the undo tablespace. Because the undo tablespace require recovery in the event of an instance or media failure, the undo from operations generates redo.

The parameter TEMP_UNDO_ENABLED has been introduced in Oracle 12c. When set to TRUE (the default), the undo information for operations against temporary tables is stored in the temporary tablespace rather than the undo tablespace. This reduces the amount of data written to the undo tablespace and eliminates the associated redo writes from the operation. The result is improved performance when using temporary tables in Oracle 12c.

Implement partitioning methods

Partitioning improves Oracle's ability to support very large tables by breaking them into smaller and more manageable pieces called partitions. Partitioned tables facilitate SQL tuning by allowing SQL statements to avoid scanning partitions that can be determined not to hold the required data using partition pruning. Partitioning can also facilitate SQL tuning by breaking down large joins of similarly-partitioned objects by using partition-wise joins. Partitioning of tables and indexes works hand-in-hand with parallel queries to improve performance in data warehouses. When an object in the database is partitioned, it is possible for parallel server processes to scan individual table partitions or index partitions when doing so makes sense.

There are three fundamental methods used to control how data is distributed into partitions: Range, Hash, and List. When partitioning data using these methods, it is possible to partition a table at a single-level, or to partition it at two levels for composite partitioning. There are advantages and design considerations for both methods. The specific needs of a given table determine which strategy is more appropriate.

Single-Level Partitioning

In single-level partitioning, a table is defined by specifying one of the following three methodologies, where one or more columns in the table act as the partitioning key:

- **Range Partitioning** -- This method maps data to partitions based on ranges of values of the partitioning key. Each of the partitions is defined with a range of values that determines which records should be placed in it. This is the most common type of partitioning and is often used with dates. Partitions are created with a VALUES LESS THAN clause, which specifies a non-inclusive upper bound for the partitions. Rows that have partitioning key values equal to or higher than this literal are added to the next higher partition. The lower bound is implied by the VALUES LESS THAN clause of the previous partition. The first partition has no lower bound. The highest partition can use a MAXVALUE literal. This represents a virtual infinite value that sorts higher than any other possible value for the partitioning key, including NULL.

- **Hash Partitioning** -- This method uses a hashing algorithm to map data to partitions using the partitioning key that you identify. The hashing algorithm is designed to evenly distribute rows among each of the partitions. This is an ideal method to distribute data evenly across devices. It is easier to implement than range partitioning. Hash partitioning is especially useful when the data to be partitioned is not historical or has no obvious partitioning key.
- **List Partitioning** -- This method allows you to specify a list of discrete values for the partitioning key in the description for each partition. In this fashion, you can control exactly how rows map to partitions. List partitioning provides the ability to group unordered and unrelated sets of data. In list partitioning, the DEFAULT partition provides a partition to store all values that are not explicitly mapped to any other partition.

Composite Partitioning

This strategy combines the basic data distribution methods. In composite partitioning, a table is partitioned by one data distribution method and then each partition is further subdivided into subpartitions using a second data distribution method. It is possible for the partitioning methods at the two levels to be the same, or different. Composite partitioning provides higher degrees of potential partition pruning and finer granularity of data placement. The possible composite partitioning methods are:

- Range-Range Partitioning
- Range-Hash Partitioning
- Range-List Partitioning
- List-Range Partitioning
- List-Hash Partitioning
- List-List Partitioning

Security

Configure the password file to use case sensitive passwords

The account passwords in the Oracle password file are case-sensitive by default. It is possible to control the case-sensitivity of the password file by using the IGNORECASE parameter when creating the password file with orapwd. By default, IGNORECASE is set to N, which means that passwords are treated as case-sensitive. The following statement creates a password file that is not case sensitive:

```
orapwd file=orapw entries=100 ignorecase=y
```

By contrast, either of the following statements creates a case-sensitive password file:

```
orapwd file=orapw entries=100 ignorecase=n
orapwd file=orapw entries=100
```

Encrypt a tablespace

It is possible to encrypt any permanent tablespace to protect sensitive data. Tablespace encryption is transparent to database users and your applications. Encrypted tablespaces are designed protect your data from unauthorized access by means <u>other</u> than through the database. This would include events such as someone getting hold of backup tapes of your database. Encrypted tablespaces also protect data from users who try to access database files directly through the operating system. When a tablespace is encrypted, all tablespace blocks are encrypted. All segment types are supported for encryption, including tables, clusters, indexes, LOBs, table and index partitions, and so on. To maximize security, data from an encrypted tablespace is automatically encrypted when written to the undo tablespace, to the redo logs, and to any temporary tablespace.

There is no disk space overhead for encrypting a tablespace. The following statement creates an encrypted tablespace with the default encryption algorithm:

```
CREATE TABLESPACE secure_ts
DATAFILE '/u02/app/oracle/oradata/orcl11g/secure01.dbf' SIZE
200M
ENCRYPTION
DEFAULT STORAGE(ENCRYPT);
```

Oracle Wallet

Tablespace encryption uses the transparent data encryption feature of Oracle Database. This feature requires that you create an Oracle Wallet to store the master encryption key for the database. The wallet must be open before you can create the encrypted tablespace and before you can store or retrieve encrypted data. When you open the wallet, it is available to all sessions. It remains open until you explicitly close it or until the database is shut down.

Encryption Algorithms

Transparent data encryption supports industry-standard encryption algorithms, including the following: 3DES168, AES128, AES192, AES256. The encryption key length is implied by the algorithm name. For example, the AES128 algorithm uses 128-bit keys. You specify the algorithm to use when you create the tablespace, and different tablespaces in the same database can use different algorithms. While longer key lengths theoretically provide greater security, there is a trade-off in CPU overhead. AES128 is the default encryption algorithm.

Restrictions

- You cannot encrypt an existing tablespace with an ALTER TABLESPACE statement.
- Encrypted tablespaces are subject to restrictions when transporting to another database.
- When recovering a database with encrypted tablespaces you must open the Oracle wallet that contains the encryption key after database mount and before database open, so the recovery process can decrypt data blocks and redo.

Configure fined grained access to network services

The Oracle database contains a set of PL/SQL utility packages, such as UTL_TCP, UTL_SMTP, UTL_MAIL, UTL_HTTP, and UTL_INADDR, which are designed to enable database users to access network services from within the database. In a default database installation, these packages are created with EXECUTE privileges granted to PUBLIC users. Prior to Oracle 11g, this meant that any user with access to an Oracle account also gained access to all of these network services. This release enhances the security of these packages by allowing database administrators the ability to restrict access to these packages.

Creating Access Control Lists

To configure fine-grained access to external network services, you create an access control list (ACL), which is stored in Oracle XML DB. It's possible to create the access control list by using Oracle XML DB itself, or by using the DBMS_NETWORK_ACL_ADMIN and DBMS_NETWORK_ACL_UTILITY PL/SQL packages.

To create the access control list by using the DBMS_NETWORK_ACL_ADMIN package, follow these steps:

First, create the Access Control List and Its Privilege Definitions via the DBMS_NETWORK_ACL_ADMIN.CREATE_ACL procedure.

```
BEGIN
  DBMS_NETWORK_ACL_ADMIN.CREATE_ACL (
    acl          => 'file_name.xml',
    description => 'file description',
    principal    => 'user_or_role',
    is_grant     => TRUE|FALSE,
    privilege    => 'connect|resolve',
    start_date   => null|timestamp_with_time_zone,
    end_date     => null|timestamp_with_time_zone);
END;
```

- **acl** -- a name for the access control list XML file.
- **description** -- a brief description of the purpose of this file.
- **principal** -- the initial user account or role being granted or denied permissions.
- **is_grant** -- either TRUE or FALSE, to indicate whether the privilege is to be granted or denied
- **privilege** -- either connect or resolve. Connect grants permission to connect to a network service. Resolve grants the user permission to resolve a network host name or an IP address.
- **start_date** --(Optional) starting date that the entry will be valid.
- **end_date** --(Optional) ending date that the entry will be valid.

Second, add additional users or roles to the access control list, or grant additional privileges to one user or role, via the DBMS_NETWORK_ACL_ADMIN.ADD_PRIVILEGE procedure.

```
BEGIN
  DBMS_NETWORK_ACL_ADMIN.ADD_PRIVILEGE (
    acl => 'file_name.xml',
    principal => 'user_or_role',
    is_grant => TRUE|FALSE,
    privilege => 'connect|resolve',
    position => null|value,
    start_date => null|timestamp_with_time_zone,
    end_date => null|timestamp_with_time_zone);
END;
```

The matching parameters that exist in ADD_PRIVILEGE and CREATE_ACL have the same meaning. The only new parameter is position, which sets the precedence for multiple users or roles.

Finally, assign the access control list to one or more network host computers using the DBMS_NETWORK_ACL_ADMIN.ASSIGN_ACL procedure. Only one access control list can be assigned to any host computer, domain, or IP subnet, and if specified, the TCP port range. When you assign a new access control list to a network target, Oracle Database unassigns the previous access control list that was assigned to the same target.

```
BEGIN
  DBMS_NETWORK_ACL_ADMIN.ASSIGN_ACL (
    acl => 'file_name.xml',
    host => 'network_host',
    lower_port => null|port_number,
    upper_port => null|port_number);
END;
```

- **acl** --the name of the access control list XML file to assign to the network host.
- **host** -- the network host to which this access control list will be assigned. This setting can be a name or IP address of the network host, or you can enter localhost.
- **lower_port** -- (Optional) For TCP connections, enter the lower boundary of the port range. Use this setting for the connect privilege only; omit it for the resolve privilege. The default is null, which means that there is no port restriction (that is, the ACL applies to all ports).
- **upper_port** -- (Optional) For TCP connections, enter the upper boundary of the port range. Use this setting for connect privileges only; omit it for resolve privileges. The default is null, which means that there is no port restriction (that is, the ACL applies to all ports).

Use Secure File LOBS to store documents with Compression, Encryption, De-duplication, Caching

In Oracle 11g, a new type of Large-Object storage was introduced, SecureFile LOBs. The legacy LOB format has been renamed to BasicFile LOBs. SecureFile LOBs add several new capabilities to LOB data storage:

- Intelligent LOB compression enables users to explicitly compress data to save disk space.
- Intelligent LOB encryption allows encrypted data to be stored in-place and is available for random reads and writes.
- The deduplication option allows Oracle to automatically detect duplicate LOB data and conserve space by only storing a single copy of the data.
- LOB data path optimization includes logical cache above storage layer, read prefetching, new caching modes, vectored IO, and more.

db_securefile parameter

The new init.ora parameter, db_securefile, is used to determine the behavior of the Oracle database in reference to using or not using SecureFile LOBs or BasicFile LOBs. The possible values of this parameter are: ALWAYS, FORCE, PERMITTED, NEVER, and IGNORE. The meaning of each of the values is:

- **ALWAYS** -- attempt to create SecureFile LOBs but fall back to BasicFile LOBs if the tablespace is not using ASSM.
- **FORCE** -- force all LOBs created going forward to be SecureFile LOBs. If the LOB is being created in an MSSM tablespace, an error will be thrown.
- **PERMITTED** -- allow SecureFile LOBs to be created
- **NEVER** -- disallow SecureFile LOBs from being created. If a DML statement tries to create a column as a SecureFile LOB, it will instead be created as a BasicFile LOB. If any SecureFile specific storage options or features are in the DML, an exception is created.

- **IGNORE** -- disallow SecureFile LOBs and ignore any errors that would otherwise be caused by forcing BasicFile LOBs with SecureFile options.

The COMPRESS, DEDUPLICATE, and ENCRYPT keywords of the CREATE TABLE statement are used to enable compression, deduplication, and encryption on SecureFile LOBs respectively. Examples of the various options follow. The first statement below creates a SecureFiles LOB column with MEDIUM compression and the second with HIGH:

```
CREATE TABLE sfltab (coll CLOB)
    LOB(coll) STORE AS SECUREFILE (
         COMPRESS
         CACHE
    );

CREATE TABLE sfltab (coll CLOB)
    LOB(coll) STORE AS SECUREFILE (
         COMPRESS HIGH
         CACHE
    );
```

The first statement below creates a SecureFiles LOB column with the deduplication option enabled and the second explicitly disables deduplication:

```
CREATE TABLE sfltab (coll CLOB)
    LOB(coll) STORE AS SECUREFILE (
        DEDUPLICATE
        CACHE
    );


CREATE TABLE sfltab (coll CLOB)
    LOB(coll) STORE AS SECUREFILE (
         KEEP_DUPLICATES
         CACHE
    );
```

Either of the two statements below will create a SecureFiles LOB column encrypted by a password key:

```
CREATE TABLE sfltab1 (col1 CLOB ENCRYPT IDENTIFIED BY [password_key])
    LOB(a) STORE AS SECUREFILE (
        CACHE
    );

CREATE TABLE sfltab (col1 CLOB)
    LOB(col1) STORE AS SECUREFILE (
        CACHE
        ENCRYPT
        IDENTIFIED BY [password_key]
    );
```

The following statement creates a SecureFiles LOB column with disabled encryption:

```
CREATE TABLE sfltab (col1 CLOB)
    LOB(col1) STORE AS SECUREFILE (
        CACHE DECRYPT
    );
```

DBMS_LOB

SecureFiles inherit the LOB column settings for deduplication, encryption, and compression that were specified at the time the LOB was created. You can use the new procedures added to the DBMS_LOB package to determine or override the inherited values.

- **DBMS_LOB.GETOPTIONS** -- The current settings of a SecureFile LOB can be obtained using this function. An integer corresponding to a pre-defined constant based on the option type is returned. As an example, the value for DEDUPLICATE_OFF is 0. You won't need to know the values for the test. You might need to know the procedure name.

- **DBMS_LOB.SETOPTIONS** -- This procedure sets features of a SecureFile LOB (compression, deduplication, and encryption). It enables the features to be set on a per-LOB basis, overriding the default LOB settings.
- **DBMS_LOB.ISSECUREFILE** -- This function returns TRUE or FALSE depending on whether the LOB locator (BLOB or CLOB) passed to it is for a SecureFile.

DBMS_SPACE.SPACE_USAGE

The existing SPACE_USAGE procedure is overloaded to return information about LOB space usage. It returns the amount of disk space in blocks used by all the LOBs in the LOB segment. This procedure can only be used on tablespaces that are created with auto segment space management.

Using Globalization Support

Customize language-dependent behavior for the database and individual sessions

National Language Support (NLS) is one of the most commonly used aspects of the Oracle database that nobody ever thinks about. The default language and location are set when an Oracle database is created. For most installations, the values are seldom changed even temporarily after that. NLS parameters can be specified in several ways:

- **Initialization parameters** -- NLS parameters can be set in the PFILE/SPFILE used by the Oracle server. Parameter file settings affect only the server behavior, not that of clients.
- **Environment variables** -- It is possible to set NLS environment variables on client machines. If set, these variables will override the server behavior for that client machine.
- **ALTER SESSION** -- The ALTER SESSION statement can be used to override the NLS behavior for a given client session.
- **SQL functions** -- NLS parameters can be explicitly set via functions in a SQL statement to hardcode NLS behavior for that statement.

The order of precedence when determining the NLS behavior is shown below. Lower numbers take precedence over higher ones (i.e. using SQL functions to explicitly set behavior will override all other methods):

1. Explicitly set in SQL functions
2. Set by an ALTER SESSION statement
3. Set as an environment variable
4. Specified in the initialization parameter file
5. Default

Some of the most commonly used NLS parameters include the following:

- **NLS_CURRENCY** -- Sets the local currency symbol.
- **NLS_DATE_FORMAT** -- Sets the default date format use by the server.
- **NLS_DATE_LANGUAGE** -- Sets the language used for day and month names.
- **NLS_LANG** -- Sets the language, territory, character set used by the database.
- **NLS_LANGUAGE** -- Sets the language used by the database.
- **NLS_SORT** -- Determines the sequence for character-based sorting.
- **NLS_TERRITORY** -- Sets the territory the database is located in.
- **NLS_TIMESTAMP_FORMAT** -- Sets the default format for timestamp data.

The NLS_LANG environment parameter is the easiest way to determine locale behavior for an Oracle Database. A single parameter can be used to set the language, territory, and the client's character set. It is set as an environment variable on UNIX platforms and the registry on Windows platforms. The NLS_LANG parameter is specified in the following format:

```
NLS_LANG = language_territory.charset
```

The default if the Oracle Universal Installer does not populate NLS_LANG is AMERICAN_AMERICA.US7ASCII. The components of the NLS_LANG parameter controls the defaults used for a number of globalization support features:

- **Language** -- This determines aspects of the server such as the language used for Oracle Database messages, character-based sorting, day names, and month names. If the language is not specified, the value defaults to AMERICAN.
- **Territory** -- This value determines behavior such as the default date, monetary, and numeric formats. If territory is not specified, the value is derived from the language value.

- **Charset** -- The charset value specifies the character set used by the client application. If charset is not specified, the value is derived from the language value.

Specify different linguistic sorts for queries

Numeric sorts are extremely simple. The numbers 3, 4, 2, and 1 can only be sorted two ways: 1-2-3-4 or 4-3-2-1. There are no language or other considerations involved in numeric sorting. By contrast character sorts can change based on the language, may or may not be case-sensitive, and can change based on accent marks on letters. There are several other considerations as well. You can reference the Oracle Database Globalization Support Guide for more details.

The Oracle Database supports several types of sorts:

- **Binary sort** -- Binary sorts use the numeric values of the characters in the character encoding scheme. This is the fastest type of sort. Both the ASCII and EBCDIC standards define the letters A to Z in ascending numeric value so a binary sort produces reasonable results for the English alphabet. However, when other languages are present, a binary sort often produces poor results.
- **Monolingual linguistic sort** -- A linguistic sort operates by replacing characters with numeric values that reflect each character's proper linguistic order. For monolingual sorts, Oracle compares character strings in two steps. First it will compare the major value of the entire string from a table of major values. Usually, letters with the same appearance have the same major value. The second step compares the minor value from a table of minor values. Both the major and minor values are defined by the Oracle Database.
- **Multilingual linguistic sort** -- Multilingual sorts are designed for operations where data in more than one language is being sorted at once. The specifics of multilingual sorts are complex. Refer to the Oracle Database Globalization Support Guide for more details. The exam is unlikely to get into the specifics of how multilingual sorts function.

The NLSSORT function can be used to perform specific linguistic sorts in an ORDER BY clause. When used, it replaces the supplied character string with an equivalent sort string. This is then used by the linguistic sort mechanism to produce the desired sorting sequence. The specific linguistic sort used by an ORDER BY clause is determined by the NLS_SORT session parameter by default. It can be explicitly overridden using the NLSSORT function. The default value of NLS_SORT is BINARY. The following statement will perform a binary sort (case-sensitive) of the characters in table ocp_emp:

```
SELECT * FROM ocp_emp ORDER BY name;
```

Query data using non-case-sensitive and accent-insensitive searches

It is possible to change the sorting to perform a case-insensitive binary sort by appending _CI to the sort type. The following example changes the NLS_SORT session value to BINARY_CI. The statement will then perform a binary sort (case-insensitive) of the characters in table ocp_emp:

```
ALTER SESSION SET NLS_SORT=BINARY_CI;
SELECT * FROM ocp_emp ORDER BY name;
```

The following example changes the NLS_SORT session value to GERMAN. The statement will then perform a German-language sort (case-sensitive) of the characters in table ocp_emp:

```
ALTER SESSION SET NLS_SORT=GERMAN;
SELECT * FROM ocp_emp ORDER BY name;
```

Linguistic sorts can also be made case-insensitive. The following example changes the NLS_SORT session value to GERMAN_CI. The statement will then perform a German-language sort (case-insensitive) of the characters in table ocp_emp:

```
ALTER SESSION SET NLS_SORT=GERMAN_CI;
SELECT * FROM ocp_emp ORDER BY name;
```

Another option is for sorts to be accent-insensitive. This is enabled by using a suffix of _AI. The following example changes the NLS_SORT session value to GERMAN_AI. The statement will then perform a German-language sort (accent-insensitive) of the characters in table ocp_emp:

```
ALTER SESSION SET NLS_SORT=GERMAN_AI;
SELECT * FROM ocp_emp ORDER BY name;
```

The session value of NLS_SORT can be overridden by using the NLSSORT function directly in the ORDER_BY clause.

```
SELECT * FROM ocp_emp
ORDER BY NLSSORT(name, 'NLS_SORT=GERMAN_AI');
```

Use datetime data types

The Oracle database has a number of data types that are designed to contain date and time information. Over the years I have seen administrators and developers who have created tables that store date information in VARCHAR2 fields rather than a DATE or TIMESTAMP field. This is certainly possible to do. A VARCHAR2 field can contain the text string '22-JUN-2014'. When that value is pulled up via a SELECT statement, it will appear to be a date to the user. However, there are numerous problems with storing dates in character fields, including:

- Unless the application has a complex parser to verify the information, invalid dates can be stored. '31-FEB-2015' and '22-JNN-2014' are both valid character strings, but invalid dates.
- Sorting the table by the field will produce a character-based sort rather than a date-based sort. For example, '01-DEC-2014' would sort as earlier than '02-JAN-1992'.

- Date arithmetic cannot be performed on character fields. Oracle cannot determine the number of days between the character data '01-SEP-2014' and '14-OCT-2014' without first converting them to a DATE data type.
- Unless the application performs rigid checking, multiple date formats might be stored in the same field (i.e. '01-MAR-2014', '01/03/2014', 'March 1st 2014').

None of these problems are a concern when date values are stored using Oracle date formats. There are four available datetime formats:

- **DATE** -- The DATE data type stores both date and time information. For each DATE value, Oracle stores the following information: century, year, month, date, hour, minute, and second.
- **TIMESTAMP** -- This is an extension of the DATE data type. It stores the year, month, and day of the DATE data type, plus hour, minute, and second values. The TIMESTAMP data type can store time to a much more granular level than the DATE data type and is useful for storing precise time values. The TIMESTAMP data type has an optional fractional seconds precision parameter that specifies the number of digits Oracle stores in the fractional part of the SECOND datetime field. The value defaults to 6, and can be a number in the range of 0 to 9.
- **TIMESTAMP WITH TIME ZONE** -- This is a variant of the TIMESTAMP data type. It includes a time zone region name or a time zone offset in its value. When a time zone offset is used, it is the difference (in hours and minutes) between local time and UTC. This data type is useful for preserving local time zone information.
- **TIMESTAMP WITH LOCAL TIME ZONE** -- This is another variant of TIMESTAMP that includes time zone information. It differs from TIMESTAMP WITH TIME ZONE in that data stored is normalized to the database time zone. Time zone information is not stored as part of the column data. When data from the column is retrieved, Oracle returns it in the user's local session time zone. This is useful when date information should always to be displayed in the time zone of the client system in a two-tier application.

The character formats that dates and time zones are displayed in are controlled by three NLS parameters. The format defined by these parameters also determines the character data that Oracle will recognize as a date and be able to implicitly convert into the appropriate DATE/TIMESTAMP data type. The three parameters are:

- **NLS_DATE_FORMAT** -- Defines the default date format to use with the TO_CHAR and TO_DATE functions. The value can be any valid date format mask.
- **NLS_TIMESTAMP_FORMAT** -- Defines the default date format for the TIMESTAMP data type.
- **NLS_TIMESTAMP_TZ_FORMAT** -- Defines the default date format for the TIMESTAMP WITH TIME ZONE and TIMESTAMP WITH LOCAL TIME ZONE data types.

The following example shows how altering the NLS_DATE_FORMAT will change the way that Oracle displays date information:

```
SELECT value
FROM   nls_session_parameters
WHERE  parameter = 'NLS_DATE_FORMAT';

VALUE
------------
DD-MON-RR

SELECT SYSDATE FROM dual;

SYSDATE
---------
22-JUN-14

ALTER SESSION SET NLS_DATE_FORMAT='DD/MM/YY';

SELECT SYSDATE FROM dual;

SYSDATE
--------
22/06/14
```

```
ALTER SESSION SET NLS_DATE_FORMAT='Month dd, yyyy';

SELECT SYSDATE FROM dual;

SYSDATE
--------------
June 22, 2014
```

Obtain globalization support configuration information

Because NLS parameters can be set at multiple levels, determining what the values are at each of the levels is important. This information allows administrators to understand how the database will respond when operations with NLS implications are performed. There are three data dictionary views that can provide information about the NLS parameters that may affect a given database session:

- **NLS_DATABASE_PARAMETERS** -- Lists permanent NLS parameters of the database.
- **NLS_INSTANCE_PARAMETERS** -- Lists NLS parameters of the instance.
- **NLS_SESSION_PARAMETERS** -- Lists NLS parameters of the user session.

The following three queries check the value of NLS_DATE_FORMAT at each of the three levels:

```
SELECT *
FROM   nls_database_parameters
WHERE  parameter = 'NLS_DATE_FORMAT';

PARAMETER          VALUE
------------------ --------------
NLS_DATE_FORMAT    DD-MON-RR
```

```
SELECT *
FROM   nls_instance_parameters
WHERE  parameter = 'NLS_DATE_FORMAT';

PARAMETER          VALUE
------------------ --------------
NLS_DATE_FORMAT


SELECT *
FROM   nls_session_parameters
WHERE  parameter = 'NLS_DATE_FORMAT';

PARAMETER          VALUE
------------------ --------------
NLS_DATE_FORMAT    DD-MON-RR
```

The value at the database level is the Oracle default. The fact that the value at the instance level is NULL indicates that NLS_DATE_FORMAT has not been set as an initialization parameter. This can be verified by querying the V$SPPARAMETER dynamic view:

```
SELECT name, value, isspecified
FROM   v$spparameter
WHERE  name = 'nls_date_format';

NAME                 VALUE       ISSPECIFIED
-------------------- ----------- ------------
nls_date_format                  FALSE
```

The session level value has been inherited from the database default. However, it is possible to change the session-level value using the ALTER SESSION command. The following example does this and checks the result:

```
ALTER SESSION SET NLS_DATE_FORMAT = 'DD-MON-YYYY';

SELECT *
FROM   nls_session_parameters
WHERE  parameter = 'NLS_DATE_FORMAT';

PARAMETER          VALUE
------------------ --------------
NLS_DATE_FORMAT    DD-MON-YYYY
```

Another useful view for obtaining NLS-related information is V$NLS_VALID_VALUES. This view contains all of the legal values for the NLS character set, sort, territory, and language. The following query shows a subset of the values available for NLS_SORT:

```
SELECT value
FROM   v$nls_valid_values
WHERE  parameter = 'SORT'

VALUE
---------------
BINARY
WEST_EUROPEAN
XWEST_EUROPEAN
GERMAN
XGERMAN
DANISH
XDANISH
SPANISH
XSPANISH
...
```

Automating Tasks with the Scheduler

Create a job, program, and schedule

The Oracle Scheduler is implemented by the procedures and functions in the DBMS_SCHEDULER package. The Scheduler enables you to control when and where various tasks occur. The Scheduler provides sophisticated, flexible enterprise scheduling functionality, which you can use to:

- **Run database program units** -- You can run PL/SQL anonymous blocks, PL/SQL stored procedures, and Java stored procedures on the local database or on remote Oracle databases.
- **Run external executables** -- You can run applications, shell scripts, and batch files, on the local system or on one or more remote systems.
- **Schedule job execution using multiple methods** -- The scheduled can employ time-based scheduling, event-based scheduling, and dependency scheduling.
- **Prioritize jobs based on business requirements** -- The Scheduler provides control over resource allocation among competing jobs.
- **Manage and monitor jobs** -- You can track information such as the status of the job and the last run time of the job by querying views using Enterprise Manager or SQL.
- **Execute and manage jobs in a clustered environment** -- The Scheduler fully supports execution of jobs in a Real Application Cluster environment.

To use the Scheduler, you create Scheduler objects. Schema objects define the what, when, and where for job scheduling. Scheduler objects enable a modular approach to managing tasks. One advantage of the modular approach is that objects can be reused when creating new tasks that are similar to existing tasks.

The principal Scheduler object is the job. A job defines the action to perform, the schedule for the action, and the location or locations where the action takes place. Most other scheduler objects are created to support jobs.

Some key points about the Oracle Scheduler:

- You may run PL/SQL and Java stored procedure, C functions, regular SQL scripts, and UNIX or Windows scripts.
- You can create time-based or event-based jobs. Events can be application-generated, scheduler-generated, or generated by a file watcher.
- The Scheduler consists of the concepts: Program, Job, Schedule, Job class, Resource group, Window and Window Group.
- The Scheduler architecture consists primarily of the job table, job coordinator, and the job workers (or slaves).

There are multiple elements of the Scheduler architecture. All except jobs are optional.

- **Programs** -- The scheduler allows you to optionally create programs which hold metadata about a task, but no schedule information. A program may relate to a PL/SQL block, a stored procedure or an OS executable file. Programs are created using the CREATE_PROGRAM procedure.
- **Schedules** -- Schedules optionally define the start time, end time and interval related to a job.
- **Jobs** -- Jobs can either be made up of predefined parts (programs and schedules) or completely self contained depending on which overload of the CREATE_JOB procedure is used to create them.
- **Job Classes** -- Job classes allow grouping of jobs with similar characteristics and resource requirements which eases administration.
- **Windows** -- Windows provide the link between the scheduler and the resource manager, allowing different resource plans to be activated at different times.
- **Window Groups** -- A window group is a collection of related windows.

Creating Jobs

```
DBMS_SCHEDULER.CREATE_JOB(
  JOB_NAME        => 'TEST_JOB1',
  JOB_TYPE        => 'PLSQL_BLOCK',
  JOB_ACTION      => 'BEGIN mytestproc; END;',
  START_DATE      => SYSTIMESTAMP,
  REPEAT_INTERVAL => 'FREQ=DAILY;INTERVAL=2',
  END_DATE        => NULL,
  COMMENTS        => 'TEST JOB')
```

- **JOB_TYPE** -- Possible values are: plsql_block, stored_procedure, executable
- **JOB_ACTION** -- Specifies the exact procedure, command, or script that the job will execute.
- **START_DATE and END_DATE** -- Specify the date that a new job should start and end. (Many jobs may not have an end_date parameter)
- **REPEAT_INTERVAL** -- You can specify a repeat interval using a PL/SQL date/time expression or a database calendaring expression.
- **COMMENTS** -- Allows you to add descriptive text to the job.

Enabling and Disabling Jobs

All jobs are disabled by default when you create them. You must explicitly enable them in order to activate and schedule them. The following examples show how to enable and disable a job.

```
DBMS_SCHEDULER.ENABLE ('TEST_JOB1')

DBMS_SCHEDULER.DISABLE ('TEST_JOB1')
```

Creating a Program

A program describes what is to be run by the Scheduler and is a separate entity from a job. A job runs at a certain time or because a certain event occurred, and calls a program. Different jobs can use the same program and run the program at different times and with different settings.

```
DBMS_SCHEDULER.CREATE_PROGRAM(
  PROGRAM_NAME   => 'UPDATE_STATS',
  PROGRAM_ACTION => 'OCPUSER.UPDATE_SCHEMA_STATS',
  PROGRAM_TYPE   => 'STORED_PROCEDURE',
  ENABLED        => TRUE)
```

Once a program exists, it a job can be created using the program component as follows:

```
DBMS_SCHEDULER.CREATE_JOB(
JOB_NAME        => 'TEST_JOB1',
PROGRAM_NAME    => 'UPDATE_STATS',
REPEAT_INTERVAL=> 'FREQ=DAILY;BYHOUR=03',
ENABLED         => TRUE)
```

Creating a Schedule

A schedule object specifies when and how many times a job is run. Schedules can be shared by multiple jobs. When you create a schedule, Oracle provides access to PUBLIC. Thus, all users can use your schedule, without any explicit grant of privileges to do so. You specify the start and end times using the TIMESTAMP WITH TIME ZONE data type. The Scheduler also supports all NLS_TIMESTAMP_TZ_FORMAT settings. You must use a calendaring expression to create the repeat interval.

```
DBMS_SCHEDULER.CREATE_SCHEDULE(
  SCHEDULE_NAME    => 'SCHEDULE_12HR',
  START_DATE       => SYSTIMESTAMP,
  END_DATE         => NULL,
  REPEAT_INTERVAL  => 'FREQ=HOURLY;INTERVAL= 12',
  COMMENTS         => 'EVERY 12 HOURS')
```

```
DBMS_SCHEDULER.CREATE_JOB(
  JOB_NAME       => 'TEST_JOB02',
  PROGRAM_NAME   => 'UPDATE_STATS',
  SCHEDULE_NAME => 'SCHEDULE_12HR')
```

Use a time-based or event-based schedule for executing Scheduler jobs

Time-Based Schedules

The DBMS_SCHEDULER.CREATE_SCHEDULE procedure allows you to define a repeating time period on which a job should be executed. Named schedules thus created can then be referenced by multiple jobs.

```
BEGIN
  DBMS_SCHEDULER.CREATE_SCHEDULE(
   schedule_name      =>  'bimonthly_15th',
   start_date         =>  SYSTIMESTAMP,
   repeat_interval    =>
'FREQ=MONTHLY;INTERVAL=2;BYMONTHDAY=15;BYHOUR=9,17;);
END;
/

BEGIN
  DBMS_SCHEDULER.CREATE_JOB (
   job_name             =>  'BIMONTHLY_ALL_HANDS',
   program_name         =>  'BIG_TIME_WASTER',
   schedule_name        =>  'BIMONTHLY_15TH'
   enabled              =>  TRUE,
   comments             =>  'my event-based job');
END;
/
```

The Scheduler job BIMONTHLY_ALL_HANDS will be executed every second month, on the 15th, at 9AM and 5PM.

Event-Based Schedules

An event is a message sent by one application or system process to another to indicate that some action or occurrence has been detected. There are three kinds of events consumed by the Scheduler:

- **Events raised by your application** -- An application can raise an event to be consumed by the Scheduler, which reacts by starting a job. For example, when an employee has been terminated, it can raise an event that starts a job to suspend the employee's access to critical systems.

- **File arrival events raised by a file watcher** -- You can create a file watcher to watch for the arrival of a file on a system. You can then configure a job to start when the file watcher detects the presence of the file.
- **Scheduler-generated events** -- The Scheduler can raise an event to indicate state changes that occur within the Scheduler itself. For example, the Scheduler can raise an event when a job starts, when a job completes, when a job stalls, and so on.

You can create a schedule that is based on an event. The schedule can then be used for multiple jobs. To do so, use the CREATE_EVENT_SCHEDULE procedure, or use Enterprise Manager. The following is an example of creating an event schedule:

```
BEGIN
  DBMS_SCHEDULER.CREATE_EVENT_SCHEDULE (
   schedule_name     =>  'EMP_TERM_EVENT_SCHEDULE',
   start_date        =>  SYSTIMESTAMP,
   event_condition   =>  'tab.employees.event_type =
''TERMINATION''',
   queue_spec        =>  'emp_events_q, emp_agent');
END;
/

BEGIN
  DBMS_SCHEDULER.CREATE_JOB (
   job_name            =>  'TERM_JOB',
   program_name        =>  'SUSPEND_ACCOUNT_ACCESS',
   schedule_name       =>  'EMP_TERM_EVENT_SCHEDULE'
   enabled             =>  TRUE,
   comments            =>  'my event-based job');
END;
/
```

The scheduler job TERM_JOB will now run whenever the TERMINATION event is raised.

Create lightweight jobs

Oracle 11g introduced the concept of lightweight jobs. In comparison with traditional DBMS_SCHEDULER jobs, lightweight jobs have lower creation overhead and generate less redo. Lightweight jobs are ideal when there is a need for a large number of short-duration jobs that run frequently. Lightweight jobs have the following characteristics:

- Unlike regular jobs, they are not schema objects.
- They have a significant improvement in create and drop time over regular jobs because they do not have the overhead of creating a schema object.
- They have lower average session creation time than regular jobs.
- They have a small footprint on disk for job metadata and runtime data.

Lightweight jobs can only be generated via a job template. You create a lightweight job by using the job_style attribute 'LIGHTWEIGHT' while creating the template. The alternative job_style is 'REGULAR', which is the default. Like programs and schedules, regular jobs are schema objects. A regular job offers more flexibility but entails more overhead when it is created or dropped. A lightweight job must reference a program object to specify a job action. The program must be enabled when the lightweight job is created, and the program type must be either 'PLSQL_BLOCK' or 'STORED_PROCEDURE'. You cannot grant privileges on lightweight jobs. They inherit privileges from the specified program. A user with privileges on the program being called has corresponding privileges on the lightweight job.

```
BEGIN
  DBMS_SCHEDULER.create_program(
    program_name   => 'lw_test',
    program_action => 'BEGIN
                         DBMS_OUTPUT.PUT_LINE(''Hello Lightweight
World'');
                       END;',
    program_type   => 'plsql_block',
    enabled        => true);
END;
/
```

```
BEGIN
DBMS_SCHEDULER.create_job (
  job_name          => 'LW_JOB_TEST',
  program_name      => 'LW_TEST',
  repeat_interval   => 'FREQ=DAILY;BYHOUR=10',
  end_date          =>  sysdate+7,
  job_style         => 'LIGHTWEIGHT',
  enabled           => TRUE,
  comments          => 'Lightweight job example');
END;
/
```

Use job chains to perform a series of related tasks

A DBMS_SCHEDULER chain is a named series of tasks that are linked together to achieve a combined objective. Chains allow you to implement dependency based scheduling. Jobs in a chain will be started depending on the outcomes of one or more previous jobs. The basic steps to create and use a chain are:

1. Create a chain object
2. Define the steps in the chain
3. Add rules
4. Enable the chain
5. Create a job that points to the chain

Creating the Chain

You create a chain by using the CREATE_CHAIN procedure.

```
BEGIN
  DBMS_SCHEDULER.CREATE_CHAIN (
     chain_name          => 'ocp_chain',
     rule_set_name       => NULL,
     evaluation_interval => NULL,
     comments            => 'Working on the chain gang');
END;
/
```

Adding Chain Steps

Once a chain object has been created, you must define one or more chain steps. Each step can point to one of the following:

- A Scheduler program object (program)
- Another chain (a nested chain)
- An event schedule or inline event

```
BEGIN
  DBMS_SCHEDULER.DEFINE_CHAIN_STEP (
     chain_name       =>  'ocp_chain1',
     step_name        =>  'ocp_step1',
     program_name     =>  'ocp_program1');
  DBMS_SCHEDULER.DEFINE_CHAIN_STEP (
     chain_name       =>  'ocp_chain1',
     step_name        =>  'ocp_step2',
     program_name     =>  'ocp_chain2');
END;
/
```

The program or chain used in the step does not have to exist during definition. It must exist and be enabled when the chain runs, or an error will be generated.

The DEFINE_CHAIN_EVENT_STEP procedure allows you to create steps that wait on events. Procedure arguments can point to an event schedule or can include an inline queue specification and event condition.

```
BEGIN
DBMS_SCHEDULER.DEFINE_CHAIN_EVENT_STEP (
   chain_name              =>  'ocp_chain1',
   step_name               =>  'ocp_step3',
   event_schedule_name     =>  'ocp_event_schedule');
END;
/
```

Adding Rules to a Chain

The DEFINE_CHAIN_RULE procedure enables you to add a rule to a chain. Chain rules define when steps are run and define dependencies between steps. Each rule has a condition and an action. If a rule's condition evaluates to TRUE, its action is performed. Conditions are usually based on the outcome of one or more previous steps. Scheduler chain condition syntax takes one of the following two forms:

```
stepname [NOT] {SUCCEEDED|FAILED|STOPPED|COMPLETED}
stepname ERROR_CODE {comparision_operator|[NOT] IN}
{integer|list_of_integers}
```

Starting and Ending the Chain

At least one rule must have a condition that always evaluates to TRUE so that the chain can start when the chain job starts. At least one chain rule must contain an action of 'END'. The following example defines a rule that starts the chain at step **step1** and a rule that starts step **step2** when **step1** completes.

```
BEGIN
DBMS_SCHEDULER.DEFINE_CHAIN_RULE (
   chain_name     =>    'ocp_chain1',
   condition      =>    'TRUE',
   action         =>    'START step1',
   rule_name      =>    'ocp_rule1',
   comments       =>    'start the chain');
DBMS_SCHEDULER.DEFINE_CHAIN_RULE (
   chain_name     =>    'ocp_chain1',
   condition      =>    'step1 completed',
   action         =>    'START step2',
   rule_name      =>    'ocp_rule2');
END;
/
```

Setting an Evaluation Interval for Chain Rules

Chain rules are evaluated at the start of the chain job and at the end of each chain step. it is also possible to configure a chain to have its rules evaluated at a repeating time interval, such as once per hour.

```
BEGIN
DBMS_SCHEDULER.CREATE_CHAIN (
   chain_name          => 'ocp_chain1',
   rule_set_name       => NULL,
   evaluation_interval => INTERVAL '30' MINUTE,
   comments            => 'Chain with 30 minute evaluation
interval');
END;
/
```

Enabling Chains

A chain must be enabled before it can be run by a job.

```
BEGIN
DBMS_SCHEDULER.ENABLE ('ocp_chain1');
END;
/
```

Creating Jobs for Chains

A chain can be initiated by the RUN_CHAIN procedure or by creating and scheduling a job of type 'CHAIN'.

```
BEGIN
DBMS_SCHEDULER.CREATE_JOB (
   job_name        => 'chain_job_1',
   job_type        => 'CHAIN',
   job_action      => 'ocp_chain1',
   repeat_interval => 'freq=daily;byhour=4;byminute=0;bysecond=0',
   enabled         => TRUE);
END;
/
```

Running Chains

You can use the RUN_CHAIN procedure to run a chain without having to first create a chain job for the chain.

```
BEGIN
DBMS_SCHEDULER.RUN_CHAIN (
   chain_name      =>  'ocp_chain1',
   job_name        =>  'ocp_chain_job');
END;
/
```

Create Windows and Job Classes

DBMS_SCHEDULER job windows link the scheduler to the Data Resource Manager. This allows different resource plans to be activated at different times. When used in conjunction with job classes (that point to resource consumer groups), windows provides control over the resources allocated to job classes during specific time periods. Only one window can be active (open) at any time, with one resource plan assigned to the window. The affect of resource plan switches is instantly visible to running jobs which are assigned to job classes. The following statement creates a window called finance_window in SYS:

```
BEGIN
  DBMS_SCHEDULER.CREATE_WINDOW (
     window_name          => 'finance_window',
     schedule_name        => 'fin_schedule',
     resource_plan        => 'fin_resourceplan',
     duration             => interval '60' minute,
     comments             => 'Finance window');
END;
/
```

Job classes allow jobs with similar characteristics to be grouped together in order to simplify administration of resource requirements. When the JOB_CLASS parameter of the CREATE_JOB procedure is left undefined, the job is assigned to the DEFAULT_JOB_CLASS. To create a job class, you use the CREATE_JOB_CLASS procedure. The following statement creates a job class called finance_jobs in SYS that uses a service called accounting and is assigned to the resource consumer group finance_group.

```
BEGIN
  DBMS_SCHEDULER.CREATE_JOB_CLASS (
   job_class_name              =>  'finance_jobs',
   resource_consumer_group     =>  'finance_group',
   service                     =>  'accounting',
   comments                    =>  'All finance jobs');
END;
/
```

Use advanced Scheduler concepts to prioritize jobs

Advanced scheduler features, such as windows, window groups, and job classes in conjunction with the Data Resource Manager, allow you to create a robust system of job schedules that will automatically adjust resource usage to fit your needs. Jobs that consume significant resources can be made to run when database usage is low. High priority jobs can be made to kick off earlier or be allocated additional resources.

The priority of any given job is not static and can change depending on when it is run. During business hours, jobs supporting application processes would have a high priority, while evenings might allocate more resources to data loads, backup operations and database maintenance processes such as refreshing materialized views. The mechanism to support resource allocation of this type is Scheduler Windows. Every window can be assigned a priority. If windows overlap, the one with the highest priority is chosen over the others because only one can be active at any given time.

Scheduler windows work in tandem with job classes to control database resource allocation. A given window specifies the resource plan that should be activated when the window opens. Job classes in turn map to a resource consumer group or to a database service, which can map to a consumer group. Any job running during a window will be granted resources based on the consumer group of its job class and the resource plan of the window. Windows have three key attributes:

- **Schedule** -- When the window is in effect.
- **Duration** -- How long the window is open.
- **Resource plan** -- The resource plan that activates when the window opens.

The following statement creates a window with low priority for jobs that should be run in the early morning hours (1AM to 5AM) on weekdays.

```
BEGIN
   DBMS_SCHEDULER.CREATE_WINDOW (
      window_name        => 'wee_hours',
      resource_plan      => 'maintenance_workload_plan',
      start_date         => '28-JAN-13 01.00.00 AM',
      repeat_interval    => 'freq=daily; byday=mon,tue,wed,thu,fri',
      duration           => interval '4' hour,
      window_priority    => 'low');
END;
/
```

Prioritizing Jobs Within a Window

When a database has a significant number of jobs -- some will be more critical than others. Assigning a priority level to jobs helps to ensure that the automatic execution of jobs fulfils your business requirements. When several jobs are to be run in a given window, each will have a set priority (which may be the default). Jobs can be given a priority at either the job or the job class level.

- Class-level prioritization is performed using resource plans.
- Job-level prioritization via the job priority attribute determines start times.

The overall priority of a given job is determined first by the resource consumer group that the job's job class is assigned to and the current resource plan. Within the job class, you can assign priority values of 1-5 to individual jobs. If two jobs in the same job class are scheduled to start at the same time, the higher priority job will take precedence. If two jobs have the same assigned priority value, the job with the earlier start date takes precedence. When no priority is assigned to a job, it defaults to 3. The following statement changes the job priority for ocp_job to a setting of 2:

```
BEGIN
  DBMS_SCHEDULER.SET_ATTRIBUTE (
   name            =>   'ocp_job',
   attribute       =>   'job_priority',
   value           =>   2);
END;
/
```

The priority of individual jobs does not transfer across job classes. If two jobs running in a given window are in different job classes, prioritization is not guaranteed. A high-priority job in one class might be started after a lower-priority job in another.

Loading and Unloading Data

Explain Data Pump architecture

Oracle Data Pump is designed to provide high-speed movement of data and metadata from one database to another. It replaces the export/import functionality that existed in earlier releases of Oracle. Data Pump is made up of three distinct parts:

- **expdp and impdp** – These are command-line clients that use the procedures provided in the DBMS_DATAPUMP package to execute export and import commands. They accept parameters entered at the command line that enable the exporting and importing of data and metadata for a complete database or for subsets of a database.
- **DBMS_DATAPUMP** – Also known as the Data Pump API, this package provides a high-speed mechanism to move all or part of the data and metadata for a site from one database to another. DBMS_DATAPUMP can be used independently of the impdp and expdp clients.
- **DBMS_METADATA** – Also known as the Metadata API, this package provides a centralized facility for the extraction, manipulation, and re-creation of dictionary metadata. DBMS_METADATA can be used independently of the impdp and expdp clients.

Data Pump jobs use a master table, a master process, and worker processes to perform the work and keep track of progress:

- **Master Table** – A master table is used to track the progress within a job while the data and metadata are being transferred. It is implemented as a user table within the database. A user performing an impdp or expdp must have the CREATE TABLE system privilege for the master table to be created plus sufficient tablespace quota. The master table will have the same name as the job that created it. A Data Pump job cannot have the same name as an existing table or view in that schema. The information in the master table is used to restart a job.

- **Master process** – A master process is created for every Data Pump Export job and Data Pump Import job. It controls the entire job, including communicating with the clients, creating and controlling a pool of worker processes, and performing logging operations.
- **Worker Process** – The master process allocates work to be executed to worker processes that perform the data and metadata processing within an operation. Data Pump can employ multiple worker processes, running in parallel, to increase job performance.

Monitor a Data Pump job

It's possible to use the Data Pump Export and Import utilities to attach to a running job. When attached in logging mode, status about the job is automatically displayed during execution in real-time. When attached using interactive-command mode, it's possible to request the job status.

Optionally, a log file can be written during the execution of a job. It summarizes the progress of the job, lists any errors, and records the completion status. You can also determine job status or to get other information about Data Pump jobs, through the Data Pump views:

- **DBA_DATAPUMP_JOBS** – Identifies all active Data Pump jobs in the database, regardless of their state, on an instance (or on all instances for RAC). It also shows all Data Pump master tables not currently associated with an active job.
- **DBA_DATAPUMP_SESSIONS** – Identifies the user sessions that are attached to a Data Pump job. The information in this view is useful for determining why a stopped Data Pump operation has not gone away.
- **V$SESSION_LONGOPS** – Data Pump operations that transfer table data (export and import) maintain an entry indicating the job progress. The entry contains the estimated transfer size and is periodically updated to reflect the actual amount of data transferred.

The V$SESSION_LONGOPS columns that are relevant to a Data Pump job are as follows:

- **USERNAME** - job owner
- **OPNAME** - job name
- **TARGET_DESC** - job operation
- **SOFAR** - megabytes transferred thus far during the job
- **TOTALWORK** - estimated number of megabytes in the job
- **UNITS** - megabytes (MB)
- **MESSAGE** - a formatted status message of the form: 'job_name: operation_name : nnn out of mmm MB done'

Use Data Pump export and import

The Data Pump Export utility is invoked using the expdp command. The actions performed by the export operation are defined by the parameters you specify. They can be supplied either on the command line or in a parameter file. Data Pump Export can be controlled using a command line, a parameter file, or an interactive-command mode.

- **Command-Line** – Enables you to specify most of the export parameters from the command line.
- **Parameter File** – Allows you to specify command-line parameters in a parameter file. The PARFILE parameter cannot be used in a parameter file, because parameter files cannot be nested.
- **Interactive-Command** – Displays an export prompt from which you can enter various commands. Some commands are specific to interactive-command mode.

Data Pump jobs manage the following types of files:

- **Dump files** – Contain the data and metadata being moved.
- **Log files** – Record the messages associated with an operation.
- **SQL files** – Record the output of a SQLFILE operation.
- **Data Files** – Files specified by the DATA_FILES parameter during a transportable import.

There are different expdp modes for unloading different portions of the database. The mode is specified using the appropriate parameter. The available modes are:

- **Full** – In a full database export, the entire database is unloaded. This mode requires the user performing the export to have the DATAPUMP_EXP_FULL_DATABASE role. Specified using the FULL parameter.
- **Schema** – This is the default export mode. If you have the DATAPUMP_EXP_FULL_DATABASE role, then you can provide a list of schemas to export. Otherwise you can export only your own schema. Specified using the SCHEMAS parameter.
- **Table** – In table mode, only a specified set of tables, partitions, and their dependent objects are unloaded. You must have the DATAPUMP_EXP_FULL_DATABASE role to export tables that are not in your own schema. Specified using the TABLES parameter.
- **Tablespace** – In tablespace mode, only the tables contained in a specified set of tablespaces are unloaded. If a table is unloaded, then its dependent objects are also unloaded. Privileged users get all tables. Unprivileged users get only the tables in their own schemas. Specified using the TABLESPACES parameter.
- **Transportable Tablespace** – In transportable tablespace mode, only the metadata for the tables (and their dependent objects) within a specified set of tablespaces is exported. The tablespace data files are copied in a separate operation. Specified using the TRANSPORT_TABLESPACES parameter.

expdp Parameters

The following parameters are applicable to expdp:

- **ATTACH** – Attaches the client session to an existing export job and automatically places you in the interactive-command interface.
- **CONTENT** – Enables you to filter what Export unloads: data only, metadata only, or both.
- **DIRECTORY** – Specifies the default location to which Export can write the dump file set and the log file.

- **DUMPFILE** – Specifies the names, and optionally, the directory objects of dump files for an export job.
- **ESTIMATE** – Specifies the method that Export will use to estimate how much disk space each table in the export job will consume (in bytes).
- **ESTIMATE_ONLY** – Instructs Export to estimate the space that a job would consume, without actually performing the export operation.
- **EXCLUDE** – Enables you to filter the metadata that is exported by specifying objects and object types to be excluded from the export operation.
- **FILESIZE** – Specifies the maximum size of each dump file.
- **FULL** – Specifies that you want to perform a full database mode export.
- **INCLUDE** – Enables you to filter the metadata that is exported by specifying objects and object types for the current export mode.
- **JOB_NAME** – Used to identify the export job in subsequent actions.
- **LOGFILE** – Specifies the name, and optionally, a directory, for the log file of the export job.
- **PARFILE** – Specifies the name of an export parameter file.
- **QUERY** – Allows you to specify a query clause that is used to filter the data that gets exported.
- **SCHEMAS** – Specifies that you want to perform a schema-mode export.
- **TABLES** – Specifies that you want to perform a table-mode export.
- **TABLESPACES** – Specifies a list of tablespace names to be exported in tablespace mode.

impdp Parameters

Many of the above parameters are also applicable to impdp. In addition, several of the more common impdp parameters are:

- **REUSE_DATAFILES** – Specifies whether the import job should reuse existing data files for tablespace creation.
- **SQLFILE** – Specifies a file into which all of the SQL DDL that Import would have executed, based on other parameters, is written.

- **STATUS** – Specifies the frequency at which the job status display is updated.
- **TABLE_EXISTS_ACTION** – Tells import what to do if the table it is trying to create already exists.
- **REMAP_DATAFILE** – Changes the name of the source data file to the target data file name in all SQL statements where the source data file is referenced.
- **REMAP_SCHEMA** – Loads all objects from the source schema into a target schema.
- **REMAP_TABLE** – Allows you to rename tables during an import operation.
- **REMAP_TABLESPACE** – Remaps all objects selected for import with persistent data in the source tablespace to be created in the target tablespace.

The following commands are applicable when using Interactive mode:

- **ADD_FILE** – Add additional dump files.
- **CONTINUE_CLIENT** – Exit interactive mode and enter logging mode.
- **EXIT_CLIENT** – Stop the import or export client session, but leave the job running.
- **KILL_JOB** – Detach all currently attached client sessions and terminate the current job.
- **PARALLEL** – Increase or decrease the number of active worker processes for the current job.
- **START_JOB** – Restart a stopped job to which you are attached.
- **STATUS** – Display detailed status for the current job and/or set status interval.
- **STOP_JOB** – Stop the current job for later restart.

Create external tables for data population

External tables are defined as tables that do not reside in the database. It's possible to have tables in any format for which an access driver is provided. Inside the Oracle data dictionary is stored metadata describing an external table. With this metadata, Oracle provides SQL access to the external table as if it were a regular database table. It's possible to perform SELECT and JOIN operations, or create views or synonyms against external tables. It is not possible to perform DML operations or create indexes on external tables.

The metadata for external tables is created using the ORGANIZATION EXTERNAL clause of the CREATE TABLE statement. An external table definition acts as a view against the external data. An access driver is mechanism by which the external data is read. Oracle Database provides two access drivers for external tables: ORACLE_LOADER and ORACLE_DATAPUMP. ORACLE_LOADER reads data from external files using the Oracle Loader technology using a subset of the control file syntax of the SQL*Loader utility. ORACLE_DATAPUMP allows you to read data from the database and insert it into an external table, and then reload it into an Oracle Database. Note that while ORACLE_DATAPUMP allows writing to external files, the functionality is not performed via DML statements. The ANALYZE statement is not supported for gathering statistics for external tables, but you can use the DBMS_STATS package. Virtual columns are not supported on external tables. For an external table, the DROP TABLE statement removes only metadata in the database. It has no effect on the actual data outside of the database.

You create external tables using the CREATE TABLE statement with an ORGANIZATION EXTERNAL clause. This statement creates only metadata in the data dictionary. The following example creates an external table using the ORACLE_LOADER access method.

```
CREATE TABLE phone_list_ext (
  employee_id       VARCHAR2(5),
  first_name        VARCHAR2(50),
  last_name         VARCHAR2(50),
  phone             VARCHAR2(20)
)
ORGANIZATION EXTERNAL (
  TYPE ORACLE_LOADER
  DEFAULT DIRECTORY ext_tables
  ACCESS PARAMETERS (
    RECORDS DELIMITED BY NEWLINE
    FIELDS TERMINATED BY ','
    MISSING FIELD VALUES ARE NULL
    (
      employee_id       CHAR(5),
      first_name        CHAR(50),
      last_name         CHAR(50),
      phone             CHAR(20)
    )
  )
  LOCATION ('phone_list.txt')
)
PARALLEL 2
REJECT LIMIT UNLIMITED;
```

The example above uses the ORACLE_LOADER access driver. This driver is used for reading text files. Essentially any file that SQL*Loader can read from can be used as an external table. The parameters in the ACCESS PARAMETERS clause are opaque to the database. These access parameters are specific to the access driver. Oracle provides these parameters to the access driver when the external table is accessed. The PARALLEL clause enables parallel query on the data sources. The REJECT LIMIT clause specifies that there is no limit on the number of errors that can occur during a query of the external data.

Only the following ALTER TABLE Clause options are allowed on external tables:

- **REJECT LIMIT** – Changes the reject limit.
- **PROJECT COLUMN REFERENCED** – The access driver processes only the columns in the select list of the query. This setting may not provide a consistent set of rows when querying a different column list from the same external table but can speed up access.
- **PROJECT COLUMN ALL** – The access driver processes all of the columns defined on the external table. This setting always provides a consistent set of rows when querying an external table. This is the default.
- **DEFAULT DIRECTORY** – Changes the default directory specification.

Managing Resources

Configure the Resource Manager

The Oracle Database Resource Manager (DRM) is designed to optimize resource allocation among concurrent database sessions. It attempts to prevent problems that can happen if the operating system makes resource decisions when presented with high overhead without having awareness of the database needs. DRM helps to overcome these problems by giving the database more control over how hardware resources are allocated. DRM enables you to classify sessions into groups based on session attributes, and then allocate resources to those groups in a way that optimizes hardware utilization for your application environment. The information that performs the functions of classifying sessions and assigning resources is called a resource plan. Oracle 11g comes with three pre-configured resource plans for DRM. There is a mixed-workload plan that provides resource management for a mixed environment consisting of both OLTP and DSS/batch jobs. There is a Data Warehouse plan that provides resource management for a data warehousing environment. Finally there is the maintenance plan that provides resource management for the maintenance window. These plans are shipped with Oracle 11g and provide resource management directives that should provide immediate benefits for the majority of database installations. There are three elements of DRM:

- **Resource consumer group**: A group of sessions that are grouped together based on resource requirements.
- **Resource plan**: A container for directives that specify how resources are allocated to resource consumer groups.
- **Resource plan directive**: Associates a resource consumer group with a particular plan and specifies how resources are to be allocated to that resource consumer group.

Resource Plan Directives

A resource plan directive for a consumer group, can specify limits for CPU and I/O resource consumption for sessions in that group. This is done by specifying the action to be taken if a call within a session exceeds one of the specified limits. These actions, called switches, occur only for sessions that are running and consuming resources, not waiting for user input or for CPU cycles. The possible actions are the following:

- The session is switched to a consumer group with lower resource allocations.
- The session is killed (terminated).
- The session's current SQL statement is aborted.

The resource plan directive attribute that determines which of the above three actions will be taken is SWITCH_GROUP. This attribute specifies the consumer group to which a session is switched if the specified criteria are met. If the value of this parameter is a consumer group, the session will be switched to that group. If the group name is 'CANCEL_SQL', the current call for that session is canceled. Finally, if the group name is 'KILL_SESSION', then the session is killed.

Per session I/O or CPU Limits

The resource plan directive attributes that can be used in specifying the criteria to use in making switch determinations follow. If not set, all default to UNLIMITED.

- **SWITCH_TIME**: Specifies the time (in CPU seconds) that a call can execute before an action is taken.
- **SWITCH_IO_MEGABYTES**: Specifies the number of megabytes of I/O that a session can transfer (read and write) before being switched.
- **SWITCH_IO_REQS**: Specifies the number of I/O requests that a session can execute before an action is taken.

Be sure you understand the meaning of and difference between the SWITCH_ESTIMATE and SWITCH_FOR_CALL CONCEPTS. These two resource plan attributes can be used to modify the behavior of resource plan switching:

- **SWITCH_ESTIMATE**: If TRUE, the database estimates the execution time of each call. If the estimated execution time exceeds SWITCH_TIME, the session is moved to the SWITCH_GROUP before beginning the call. The default is FALSE.
- **SWITCH_FOR_CALL**: If TRUE, a session that was automatically switched to another consumer group is returned to its original consumer group when the top level call completes. The default is NULL.

The CREATE_SIMPLE_PLAN procedure of the DBMS_RESOURCE_MANAGER package allows a relatively easy way to create a basic resource management plan. A single call can be used to create up to eight consumer groups and allocate resources to them. The procedure supports only the EMPHASIS CPU application method and consumer groups use the ROUND_ROBIN scheduling policy. Consumer groups specified in the procedure are allocated CPU percentages at Level 2. The procedure implicitly includes the SYS_GROUP in the created plan and allocates 100% of the Level 1 CPU to it. It also includes the OTHER_GROUPS consumer group and allocates 100% of the Level 3 CPU to it.

The CREATE_SIMPLE_PLAN procedure contains the following arguments:

- **SIMPLE_PLAN** -- Name of the plan
- **CONSUMER_GROUP1** -- Consumer group name for first group
- **GROUP1_PERCENT** -- CPU resource allocated to this group
- **CONSUMER_GROUP2** -- Consumer group name for second group
- **GROUP2_PERCENT** -- CPU resource allocated to this group
- **CONSUMER_GROUP3** -- Consumer group name for third group
- **GROUP3_PERCENT** -- CPU resource allocated to this group
- **CONSUMER_GROUP4** -- Consumer group name for fourth group
- **GROUP4_PERCENT** -- CPU resource allocated to this group

- **CONSUMER_GROUP5** -- Consumer group name for fifth group
- **GROUP5_PERCENT** -- CPU resource allocated to this group
- **CONSUMER_GROUP6** -- Consumer group name for sixth group
- **GROUP6_PERCENT** -- CPU resource allocated to this group
- **CONSUMER_GROUP7** -- Consumer group name for seventh group
- **GROUP7_PERCENT** -- CPU resource allocated to this group
- **CONSUMER_GROUP8** -- Consumer group name for eighth group
- **GROUP8_PERCENT** -- CPU resource allocated to this group

The following statement creates a resource plan with three groups and allocates a percentage of the Level2 CPU to each.

```
BEGIN
  DBMS_RESOURCE_MANAGER.CREATE_SIMPLE_PLAN(
      SIMPLE_PLAN      => 'OCPREP_SIMPLE',
      CONSUMER_GROUP1 => 'OCPGROUP1', GROUP1_PERCENT => 50,
      CONSUMER_GROUP2 => 'OCPGROUP2', GROUP2_PERCENT => 30,
      CONSUMER_GROUP2 => 'OCPGROUP3', GROUP3_PERCENT => 20);
END;
```

Create resource plans within groups

Complex resource plans are defined as any plan that is not created using the CREATE_SIMPLE_PLAN procedure. That said, it is possible to create some extremely complex plans using DBMS_RESOURCE_MANAGER. Resource plans can cause a single user session to jump back and forth between multiple consumer groups as its resource usage changes.

The full capabilities of DRM are beyond the scope of the exam (and this guide). The example presented is a plan that is complex enough to familiarize you with a number of the DRM calls. In the example below, only two consumer groups are created, START_HERE and BAD_SQL_NO_BISCUIT. Sessions begin in the START_HERE group. If a query takes more than 10 minutes of CPU time, it is switched to the BAD_SQL_NO_BISCUIT consumer group with a maximum utilization limit of 15%. This limits the amount of resources that they can consume until a DBA intervenes.

```
BEGIN
  DBMS_RESOURCE_MANAGER.CREATE_PENDING_AREA();

  DBMS_RESOURCE_MANAGER.CREATE_CONSUMER_GROUP (
     CONSUMER_GROUP => 'START_HERE',
     COMMENT        => 'Sessions start here');

  DBMS_RESOURCE_MANAGER.CREATE_CONSUMER_GROUP (
     CONSUMER_GROUP => 'BAD_SQL_NO_BISCUIT',
     COMMENT        => 'Sessions switched here to punish bad SQL');

  DBMS_RESOURCE_MANAGER.CREATE_PLAN(
    PLAN    => 'No_Biscuit',
    COMMENT => 'Find bad queries. Swat bad queries.');

  DBMS_RESOURCE_MANAGER.CREATE_PLAN_DIRECTIVE(
    PLAN                  => 'No_Biscuit',
    GROUP_OR_SUBPLAN      => 'START_HERE',
    COMMENT               => 'Max CPU 10 minutes before switch',
    MGMT_P1               => 75,
    switch_group          => 'BAD_SQL_NO_BISCUIT',
    switch_time           => 600);

  DBMS_RESOURCE_MANAGER.CREATE_PLAN_DIRECTIVE(
    PLAN                  => 'No_Biscuit',
    GROUP_OR_SUBPLAN      => 'OTHER_GROUPS',
    COMMENT               => 'Mandatory',
    MGMT_P1               => 25);

  DBMS_RESOURCE_MANAGER.CREATE_PLAN_DIRECTIVE(
    PLAN                  => 'No_Biscuit',
    GROUP_OR_SUBPLAN      => 'BAD_SQL_NO_BISCUIT',
    COMMENT               => 'Limited CPU',
    MGMT_P2               => 100,
    MAX_UTILIZATION_LIMIT => 15);

  DBMS_RESOURCE_MANAGER.VALIDATE_PENDING_AREA();
  DBMS_RESOURCE_MANAGER.SUBMIT_PENDING_AREA();
END;
/
```

Assign users to Resource Manager groups

In order to make effective use of a Resource Manager plan, administrators must define which groups that databases users will belong to. The initial consumer group is the one to which any session created by that user will initially belong to.

If a user has not had an initial consumer group set, their initial consumer group will be the consumer group: DEFAULT_CONSUMER_GROUP. The DEFAULT_CONSUMER_GROUP has switch privileges granted to PUBLIC, so all users have the switch privilege for it. When a consumer group is deleted, any users who had that group as their initial consumer group will have DEFAULT_CONSUMER_GROUP as their initial consumer group. If there are active sessions at the time a consumer group is deleted, they are immediately switched to DEFAULT_CONSUMER_GROUP.

The initial consumer group is set by the SET_INITIAL_CONSUMER_GROUP procedure of the DBMS_RESOURCE_MANAGER package. The syntax for this procedure is:

```
DBMS_RESOURCE_MANAGER.SET_INITIAL_CONSUMER_GROUP (
   user           IN VARCHAR2,
   consumer_group IN VARCHAR2);
```

The following example sets the initial consumer group for GJONES to START_HERE:

```
BEGIN
  DBMS_RESOURCE_MANAGER.SET_INITIAL_CONSUMER_GROUP (
     'GJONES',
     'START_HERE');
END;
```

Specify directives for allocating resources to consumer groups

Plan directives are the heart of resource management. They define the boundaries and behavior that ensure system resources are restricted in a predictable fashion. The CREATE_PLAN_DIRECTIVE procedure of the DBMS_RESOURCE_MANAGER package is used to create directives. This procedure has a huge number of parameters, but generally only a few of the parameters are used for creating a single directive. The procedure is:

```
DBMS_RESOURCE_MANAGER.CREATE_PLAN_DIRECTIVE (
  plan                          IN VARCHAR2,
  group_or_subplan              IN VARCHAR2,
  comment                       IN VARCHAR2,
  cpu_p1                        IN NUMBER DEFAULT NULL, -- deprecated
  cpu_p2                        IN NUMBER DEFAULT NULL, -- deprecated
  cpu_p3                        IN NUMBER DEFAULT NULL, -- deprecated
  cpu_p4                        IN NUMBER DEFAULT NULL, -- deprecated
  cpu_p5                        IN NUMBER DEFAULT NULL, -- deprecated
  cpu_p6                        IN NUMBER DEFAULT NULL, -- deprecated
  cpu_p7                        IN NUMBER DEFAULT NULL, -- deprecated
  cpu_p8                        IN NUMBER DEFAULT NULL, -- deprecated
  active_sess_pool_p1           IN NUMBER DEFAULT NULL,
  queueing_p1                   IN NUMBER DEFAULT NULL,
  parallel_degree_limit_p1      IN NUMBER DEFAULT NULL,
  switch_group                  IN VARCHAR2 DEFAULT NULL,
  switch_time                   IN NUMBER DEFAULT NULL,
  switch_estimate               IN BOOLEAN DEFAULT FALSE,
  max_est_exec_time             IN NUMBER DEFAULT NULL,
  undo_pool                     IN NUMBER DEFAULT NULL,
  max_idle_time                 IN NUMBER DEFAULT NULL,
  max_idle_blocker_time         IN NUMBER DEFAULT NULL,
  switch_time_in_call           IN NUMBER DEFAULT NULL, -- deprecated
  mgmt_p1                       IN NUMBER DEFAULT NULL,
  mgmt_p2                       IN NUMBER DEFAULT NULL,
  mgmt_p3                       IN NUMBER DEFAULT NULL,
  mgmt_p4                       IN NUMBER DEFAULT NULL,
  mgmt_p5                       IN NUMBER DEFAULT NULL,
  mgmt_p6                       IN NUMBER DEFAULT NULL,
  mgmt_p7                       IN NUMBER DEFAULT NULL,
  mgmt_p8                       IN NUMBER DEFAULT NULL,
  switch_io_megabytes           IN NUMBER DEFAULT NULL,
  switch_io_reqs                IN NUMBER DEFAULT NULL,
  switch_for_call               IN BOOLEAN DEFAULT NULL,
  max_utilization_limit         IN NUMBER DEFAULT NULL,
  parallel_target_percentage IN NUMBER DEFAULT NULL,
  parallel_queue_timeout        IN NUMBER DEFAULT NULL);
```

The descriptions of the parameters are:

- **plan** -- Name of the resource plan
- **group_or_subplan** -- Name of the consumer group or subplan
- **comment** -- Comment for the plan directive
- **cpu_p1 to p8** -- deprecated: use mgmt_p1 to p8 instead
- **active_sess_pool_p1** -- Specifies maximum number of concurrently active sessions for a consumer group.
- **queueing_p1** -- Specified time (in seconds) after which a job in the inactive session queue (waiting for execution) will time out.
- **parallel_degree_limit_p1** -- Specifies a limit on the degree of parallelism for any operation.
- **switch_group** -- Specifies consumer group to switch to, once a switch condition is met. If the group name is 'CANCEL_SQL', then the current call is canceled when the switch condition is met. If the group name is 'KILL_SESSION', then the session is killed when the switch condition is met. Default is NULL.
- **switch_time** -- Specifies time (in CPU seconds) that a session can execute before an action is taken.
- **switch_estimate** -- If TRUE, tells Oracle to use its execution time estimate to automatically switch the consumer group of an operation before beginning its execution. Default is FALSE.
- **max_est_exec_time** -- Specifies the maximum execution time (in CPU seconds) allowed for a session. If the optimizer estimates that an operation will take longer than MAX_EST_EXEC_TIME, the operation is not started and ORA-07455 is issued. If the optimizer does not provide an estimate, this directive has no effect.
- **undo_pool** -- Limits the size in kilobytes of the undo records corresponding to uncommitted transactions by this consumer group.
- **max_idle_time** -- Indicates the maximum session idle time.
- **max_idle_blocker_time** -- Maximum amount of time in seconds that a session can be idle while blocking another session's acquisition of a resource switch_time_in_call. This parameter is deprecated. When specified, switch_time is set to switch_time_in_call (in seconds) and switch_for_ call is effectively set to TRUE. It is better to use switch_time and switch_for_call.
- **mgmt_p1 to p8** -- Resource allocation value for level 1 to 8 (replaces cpu_p1 to p8).

- **switch_io_megabytes** -- Specifies the amount of I/O (in MB) that a session can issue before an action is taken.
- **switch_io_reqs** -- Specifies the number of I/O requests that a session can issue before an action is taken.
- **switch_for_call** -- Specifies that if an action is taken because of the switch_time, switch_io_megabytes, or switch_io_reqs parameters, the consumer group is restored to its original consumer group at the end of the top call. Default is FALSE, which means that the original consumer group is not restored at the end of the top call.
- **max_utilization_limit** -- Specifies the maximum percentage of CPU that this Consumer Group or Sub-Plan can utilize. Valid values are 0% to 100%. NULL implies that there is no limit, or equivalently 100%.
- **parallel_target_percentage** -- Specifies the maximum percentage of the target number of parallel servers in an Oracle RAC environment that a consumer group can use. Any additional parallel statements
- **parallel_queue_timeout** -- Specifies the time (in seconds) that a query may remain in its Consumer Group's parallel statement queue before it is removed and terminated with an error (ORA-07454).

The sample resource plan from the earlier chapter included three plan directives. The first statement allocates 75% of the level 1 CPU resources to the START_HERE group. If a query for a user in this resource group runs for more than 10 minutes (600 seconds), it will be switched to the BAD_SQL_NO_BISCUIT consumer group.

```
DBMS_RESOURCE_MANAGER.CREATE_PLAN_DIRECTIVE(
  PLAN                    => 'No_Biscuit',
  GROUP_OR_SUBPLAN        => 'START_HERE',
  COMMENT                 => 'Max CPU 10 minutes before switch',
  MGMT_P1                 => 75,
  switch_group            => 'BAD_SQL_NO_BISCUIT',
  switch_time             => 600);
```

The second statement created a directive that assigned the remaining 25% of the level 1 CPU resources to OTHER_GROUPS. Any session that is *not* in the START_HERE or BAD_SQL_NO_BISCUIT will use this directive. There is no switch_group defined for this directive, so users will not be switched to another group for excessive resource use.

```
DBMS_RESOURCE_MANAGER.CREATE_PLAN_DIRECTIVE(
  PLAN                     => 'No_Biscuit',
  GROUP_OR_SUBPLAN         => 'OTHER_GROUPS',
  COMMENT                  => 'Mandatory',
  MGMT_P1                  => 25);
```

The third directive defines the resources for the BAD_SQL_NO_BISCUIT consumer group. Sessions in this group will be allocated 100% of the Level 2 CPU resources. A single user in this group can utilize a maximum of 15% of the available CPU resources.

```
DBMS_RESOURCE_MANAGER.CREATE_PLAN_DIRECTIVE(
  PLAN                     => 'No_Biscuit',
  GROUP_OR_SUBPLAN         => 'BAD_SQL_NO_BISCUIT',
  COMMENT                  => 'Limited CPU',
  MGMT_P2                  => 100,
  MAX_UTILIZATION_LIMIT => 15);
```

Managing Database Performance

Use the SQL Tuning Advisor

The SQL Tuning Advisor is the Oracle optimizer working in a different capacity. The optimizer has the ability to run in two different modes as described below:

- **Normal mode** – The optimizer compiles the SQL and generates an execution plan. This mode generates a reasonable plan for the vast majority of SQL statements. When running in normal mode, the output of the optimizer is an execution plan and is generally returned within a fraction of a second.
- **Tuning mode** – In this mode additional analysis is performed in an attempt to improve the plan produced in normal mode. The output from the optimizer is a set of suggested actions for producing a significantly better plan. The results from the optimizer in tuning mode can take several minutes to complete and are therefore not practical to use for routine generation of execution plans.

SQL Tuning Advisor can be invoked manually for tuning one or more SQL statements. A SQL Tuning Set (STS) is required to tune multiple statements. SQL Tuning Advisor can make use of the SQL from several different sources, including:

- **Automatic Database Diagnostic Monitor** -- This is the default source. ADDM analyzes key statistics gathered by the Automatic Workload Repository to identify any performance problems including high-load SQL statements.
- **Automatic Workload Repository** -- AWR snapshots of system activity include high-load SQL statements. These SQL statements are ranked by relevant statistics, such as CPU consumption and wait time. You can tune any high-load SQL that ran within the retention period of AWR using SQL Tuning Advisor.
- **Shared SQL area** -- You can use the shared SQL area to tune recent SQL statements that have yet to be captured in the AWR.

- **SQL tuning set** -- A SQL tuning set (STS) is a database object that stores SQL statements along with their execution context. An STS can include SQL statements that are not yet deployed in production.

You can manage the scope and duration of a SQL Tuning Advisor tuning task. The scope of a tuning task can be either of the following:

- **Limited** -- SQL Tuning Advisor will produce recommendations based on statistical checks, access path analysis, and SQL structure analysis. SQL profile recommendations will not be generated.
- **Comprehensive** -- SQL Tuning Advisor carries out all the analysis from the limited scope plus SQL Profiling. When using the comprehensive option, a time limit can be specified for the tuning task. The default is 30 minutes.

Advisor Output

Once SQL Tuning Advisor has analyzed the SQL statement(s), it will return the following:

- Information on optimizing the execution plan.
- The rationale for the proposed optimization.
- The estimated performance benefit.
- The command to implement the advice.

You make the decision on whether or not to implement the recommendations. Oracle recommends using the Enterprise Manager interface for running SQL Tuning Advisor. If EM is unavailable, then you can run SQL Tuning Advisor using procedures in the DBMS_SQLTUNE package. Using SQL Tuning Advisor via the DBMS_SQLTUNE package is a multi-step process:

1. Create a SQL tuning set (if tuning multiple SQL statements)
2. Create a SQL tuning task
3. Execute a SQL tuning task
4. Display the results of a SQL tuning task
5. Implement recommendations as appropriate

SQL Tuning Tasks

A tuning task can be created using the text of a single SQL statement, a SQL tuning set with multiple statements, a SQL statement selected by SQL identifier from the shared SQL area, or a SQL statement selected by SQL identifier from AWR. The following example uses SQL Tuning Advisor to optimize a specified SQL statement text.

```
DECLARE
  v_task_name    VARCHAR2(30);
  v_sqltext      CLOB;
BEGIN
  v_sqltext := 'SELECT first_name, last_name ' ||
               'FROM   hr.employees e ' ||
               '       INNER JOIN hr.departments d ' ||
               '       ON e.department_id = d.department_id ' ||
               '       INNER JOIN hr.locations l ' ||
               '       ON l.location_id = d.location_id ' ||
               'WHERE  e.employee_id < :bindvar';

  v_task_name := DBMS_SQLTUNE.CREATE_TUNING_TASK(
                sql_text    => v_sqltext,
                bind_list   => sql_binds(anydata.ConvertNumber(100)),
                user_name   => 'HR',
                scope       => 'COMPREHENSIVE',
                time_limit  => 45,
                task_name   => 'oce_tuning_task',
                description => 'Example Tuning Task');
END;
/
```

Once the tuning task has been created, the task is executed to start the tuning process:

```
BEGIN
  DBMS_SQLTUNE.EXECUTE_TUNING_TASK( task_name => 'oce_tuning_task' );
END;
/
```

The status of a task is available in the USER_ADVISOR_TASKS view:

```
SELECT status
FROM   user_advisor_tasks
WHERE  task_name = 'oce_sql_tuning_task';
```

The execution progress of the task is available in the V$ADVISOR_PROGRESS view:

```
SELECT sofar, totalwork
FROM   v$advisor_progress
WHERE  user_name = 'HR'
AND    task_name = 'oce_sql_tuning_task';
```

Once the task has completed, you display a report of the findings and recommendations. For each proposed recommendation, the rationale and benefit is provided along with the SQL statements needed to implement the recommendation. The report is generated with the REPORT_TUNING_TASK function of DBMS_SQLTUNE:

```
SET LONG 1000
SET LONGCHUNKSIZE 1000
SET LINESIZE 100
SELECT DBMS_SQLTUNE.REPORT_TUNING_TASK(
       'oce_sql_tuning_task')
FROM   DUAL;
```

You can use the following APIs for managing SQL tuning tasks:

- **INTERRUPT_TUNING_TASK** -- This will interrupt a task while executing, causing a normal exit with intermediate results.
- **RESUME_TUNING_TASK** -- This will resume a previously interrupted task.
- **CANCEL_TUNING_TASK** -- This will cancel a task while executing, removing all results from the task.
- **RESET_TUNING_TASK** -- This will reset a task while executing, removing all results from the task and returning the task to its initial state.
- **DROP_TUNING_TASK** -- This will drop a task, removing all results associated with it.

Use the SQL Access Advisor to tune a workload

The SQL Access Advisor is designed to help make sure that an efficient path to the data exists. SQL Access advisor offers recommendations intended to achieve the proper set of materialized views, materialized view logs, and indexes for a given workload. As a general rule, as the number of materialized views and indexes increase, query performance improves. SQL Access Advisor weighs trade-offs between space usage and query performance. SQL Access Advisor makes recommendations, each of which will contain one or more actions. If a recommendation contains multiple actions, all of the individual actions must be implemented to achieve the full benefit. If the advisor decides that one or more base tables should be partitioned, it will collect all individual partition actions into a single recommendation. In that case, note that some or all of the remaining recommendations might be dependent on implementing the partitioning recommendation. It is not possible to view index and materialized view advice in isolation of the underlying table's partitioning.

The SQL Access Advisor API can perform the following functions:

- Recommend materialized views and indexes based on collected, user-supplied, or hypothetical workload information.
- Recommend partitioning of tables, indexes, and materialized views.
- Mark, update, and remove recommendations.
- Perform a quick tune using a single SQL statement.
- Show how to make a materialized view fast refreshable.
- Show how to change a materialized view so that general query rewrite is possible.

The SQL Access Advisor relies on structural statistics about table and index cardinalities of dimension level columns, JOIN KEY columns, and fact table key columns. If these statistics are missing for a given table, queries referencing this table are marked as invalid in the workload. SQL Access Advisor will make no recommendations for those queries. Prior to running SQL Access Advisor, you should also ensure that existing indexes and materialized views have been analyzed.

Modes of Operation

SQL Access Advisor has two modes of operation: problem solving and evaluation. The default mode is problem solving. In this mode, SQL Access Advisor will attempt to solve access method problems by looking for new objects to create. When operating in evaluation mode, SQL Access Advisor will only comment on existing access paths that the given workload will use. A problem solving run might recommend creating a new index whereas an evaluation only scenario will only produce recommendations such as retaining an existing index. The evaluation mode is useful in determining which indexes and materialized views are actually being used by a given workload.

Intermediate Results

With 11g, SQL Access Advisor allows you to see intermediate results during the analysis operation. Previously, results were unavailable until the processing had completed or was interrupted by the user. With the change, it is possible to access results in the recommendation and action tables while the SQL Access Advisor task is still executing. Intermediate results represent recommendations only for the portion of the workload that has been executed up to that point in time. If the entire workload must be evaluated, then you should allow the task to complete normally. Recommendations made by the advisor early in the evaluation process will not have any base table partitioning recommendations. Partitioning analysis requires most of the workload to be processed before it's clear whether partitioning would be beneficial.

Creating Tasks

You create advisor tasks to define what it is you want to analyze and where the analysis results should be placed. It's possible to create any number of tasks, each with a given specialization. All are based on the same Advisor task model and share the same repository. Tasks are created using the CREATE_TASK procedure:

```
VARIABLE task_id NUMBER;
VARIABLE task_name VARCHAR2(255);
EXECUTE :task_name := 'MYTASK';
EXECUTE DBMS_ADVISOR.CREATE_TASK
         ('SQL Access Advisor', :task_id, :task_name);
```

SQL Tuning Sets

The input workload for the SQL Access Advisor is the SQL Tuning Set. An important benefit of using a SQL Tuning Set is that because SQL Tuning Sets are stored as separate entities, they can be referenced by many Advisor tasks. A workload reference will be removed when a parent Advisor task is deleted or when the workload reference is removed from the Advisor task by the user. A SQL Tuning Set workload is created using DBMS_SQLTUNE. You can pull SQL Workload objects into a SQL Tuning Set using DBMS_ADVISOR:

```
EXECUTE DBMS_ADVISOR.COPY_SQLWKLD_TO_STS('MYWORKLOAD','MYSTS','NEW');
```

Linking Tasks and Workloads

Tasks must be linked to a SQL Tuning Set in order to generate advisor recommendations. You create links with the ADD_STS_REF procedure, using their respective names to link the task to a Tuning Set. Once a connection has been defined, the SQL Tuning Set is protected from removal or update.

```
EXECUTE DBMS_ADVISOR.ADD_STS_REF('MYTASK', null, 'MYWORKLOAD');
```

Removing a Link

Before a task or a SQL Tuning Set workload can be deleted, any existing links between the task and the workload must be removed. Links are removed using the DELETE_STS_REF procedure.

```
EXECUTE DBMS_ADVISOR.DELETE_STS_REF('MYTASK', null, 'MYWORKLOAD');
```

Recommendation Options

Parameters for a given task must be defined using the SET_TASK_PARAMETER procedure before recommendations can be generated. If parameters are not defined, then the defaults are used. You can set task parameters by using the SET_TASK_PARAMETER procedure.

```
DBMS_ADVISOR.SET_TASK_PARAMETER (
          task_name IN VARCHAR2,
          parameter IN VARCHAR2,
          value IN [VARCHAR2 | NUMBER]);
```

Generating Recommendations

You can generate recommendations by using the EXECUTE_TASK procedure. After it completes, the DBA_ADVISOR_LOG table will show execution status and the number of recommendations and actions produced. EXECUTE_TASK is a synchronous operation, so control will not be returned to the user until the operation has completed, or is interrupted. Upon completion, you can check the DBA_ADVISOR_LOG table for the execution status. The recommendations can be queried by task name in DBA_ADVISOR_RECOMMENDATIONS and the actions in DBA_ADVISOR_ACTIONS.

```
EXECUTE DBMS_ADVISOR.EXECUTE_TASK('MYTASK');
```

Use Database Replay

Oracle Database Replay captures all external database calls made to the system during the workload capture period. The capture includes all relevant information about the client request, such as SQL text, bind values, and transaction information. Background activities of the database and scheduler jobs are not captured. In addition, the following types of client requests are not captured in a workload:

- Direct path load of data from external files using utilities such as SQL*Loader
- Shared server requests (Oracle MTS)
- Oracle Streams
- Advanced replication streams
- Non-PL/SQL based Advanced Queuing (AQ)
- Flashback queries
- Oracle Call Interface (OCI) based object navigations
- Non SQL-based object access
- Distributed transactions

It is a best practice to restart the database before capturing the production workload. This ensures that ongoing and dependent transactions are allowed to be completed or rolled back before the capture begins. If the database is not restarted before the capture, transactions that are in progress or have yet to be committed will be only partially captured in the workload.

By default, all activities from all user sessions are recorded during workload capture. Workload filters can be used to include or exclude specific user sessions during the workload capture. You can use either inclusion filters or exclusion filters in a workload capture, but not both simultaneously. Inclusion filters specify user sessions that will be captured in the workload. Exclusion filters enable you to specify user sessions that will not be captured in the workload. To add filters to a workload capture, you use the DBMS_WORKLOAD_CAPTURE.ADD_FILTER procedure. To remove an existing filter, you use the DBMS_WORKLOAD_CAPTURE.DELETE_FILTER procedure.

You should have a well-defined starting point for the workload so that the database being used to replay the workload can be restored to the same point before starting the captured workload. It is best not to have any active user sessions when starting a workload capture. Active sessions may have ongoing transactions which will not be replayed completely. Consider restarting the database in RESTRICTED mode prior to starting the workload capture. When the workload capture begins, the database will automatically switch to UNRESTRICTED mode and normal operations can continue while the workload is being captured. You begin a workload capture using the procedure DBMS_WORKLOAD_CAPTURE.START_CAPTURE. To stop a workload capture in progress, you use the DBMS_WORKLOAD_CAPTURE.FINISH_CAPTURE procedure.

You can export AWR data from the production machine in order to enable detailed analysis of the workload on both systems. This data is required if you plan to run the AWR Compare Period report on a pair of workload captures or replays. To export AWR data, you use the DBMS_WORKLOAD_CAPTURE.EXPORT_AWR procedure.

The following views allow you to monitor a workload capture. You can also use Oracle Enterprise Manager to monitor a workload capture:

- **DBA_WORKLOAD_CAPTURES** -- Lists all the workload captures that have been created in the current database.
- **DBA_WORKLOAD_FILTERS** -- Lists all workload filters used for workload captures defined in the current database.

After the workload has been captured, it's necessary to preprocess the capture files prior to using them in a replay. Preprocessing converts the captured data into replay files and creates the required metadata needed to replay the workload. After preprocessing the captured workload, it can be replayed multiple times on any replay system running the same version of Oracle. As a general rule, it's recommended to move the capture files to another system for preprocessing. While the capture itself has a minimal overhead, workload preprocessing can be time consuming and resource intensive. It is better that this step be performed on the test system where the workload will be replayed rather than on the production database. Capture files are processed using the DBMS_WORKLOAD_REPLAY.PROCESS_CAPTURE procedure.

After you have preprocessed a captured workload, it can be replayed on the test system. In the workload replay, Oracle will perform the actions recorded during the workload capture. It will re-create all captured external client requests with the same timing, concurrency, and transaction dependencies that occurred on the production system. Database Replay uses a program called the replay client to re-create the external client requests. You may need to use multiple replay clients depending on the scope of the captured workload. The replay client has an imbedded calibration tool to help determine the number of replay clients required for a given workload. The entire workload from the production database is replayed. This includes DML and SQL queries, so the data in the replay system must be as logically similar to the data in the capture system as possible.

Gather and use optimizer statistics

Starting with the 11g Release, it is possible to automatically publish the statistics at the end of the gather operation (the default behavior), or to have the new statistics be saved as pending. When saved as pending, you can validate the new statistics and publish them only if they generate acceptable optimizer plans. The following command will return 'TRUE' if statistics will be published when they are gathered, or FALSE if the statistics will be kept pending.

```
SELECT DBMS_STATS.GET_PREFS('PUBLISH') publish
FROM  dual;
```

You can change the PUBLISH setting at either the schema or the table level. By default, the optimizer uses only published statistics in generating plans. If you want the optimizer to use pending statistics, you may set the initialization parameter **OPTIMIZER_USE_PENDING_STATISTICS** to TRUE (the default value is FALSE). You may publish pending stats for a single table, single schema, or the entire database with the DBMS_STATS.PUBLISH_PENDING_STATS procedure;

- **Database** - DBMS_STATS.PUBLISH_PENDING_STATS (NULL, NULL);
- **Schema** - DBMS_STATS.PUBLISH_PENDING_STATS (schema_name, NULL);
- **Table** - DBMS_STATS.PUBLISH_PENDING_STATS (schema_name, table_name);

GRANULARITY AND INCREMENTAL parameters

For partitioned tables and indexes, DBMS_STATS can gather separate statistics for each partition and global statistics for the entire table or index. The type of partitioning statistics to be gathered is specified in the GRANULARITY argument of the DBMS_STATS gathering procedures. Both types can be important for creating good plans. Oracle recommends setting the GRANULARITY parameter to AUTO to gather both types of partition statistics.

With partitioned tables, new data is often loaded into a new partition. As new partitions are added and data loaded, statistics must be gathered on the new partition, and global statistics must be kept up to date for the entire table. If the INCREMENTAL value for a partition table is set to TRUE, and you gather statistics on that table with the GRANULARITY parameter set to AUTO, Oracle will gather statistics on the new partition and update the global table statistics by scanning only those partitions that have been modified rather than the entire table. If the INCREMENTAL value for the partitioned table is set to FALSE (the default value), then a full table scan is used to maintain the global statistics. This is a highly resource intensive and time consuming operation for large tables. Setting INCREMENTAL to TRUE for a partitioned table requires the SYSAUX tablespace to consume additional space to maintain the global statistics.

New sampling technique

Gathering statistics for a large table can be very time-consuming if the operation reads every row. Sampling a small percentage of the rows provides a much faster operation, albeit with less reliable metrics. The sample size is specified using the ESTIMATE_PERCENT argument of the DBMS_STATS procedures. Prior to 11g, this value has been set to a static value, commonly 5, 10, or 15%. With 11g, Oracle recommends setting the parameter to the new function DBMS_STATS.AUTO_SAMPLE_SIZE. This new function is designed to maximize performance gains while achieving necessary statistical accuracy. AUTO_SAMPLE_SIZE lets Oracle determine the best sample size necessary for good statistics, based on the statistical properties of the particular object.

Multi-Column Statistics

When multiple columns from a single table are used together in the where clause of a query, the relationship between the columns can strongly affect the combined selectivity for the column group. For example, consider a table that has city and state columns. Selecting city and state together produces a much smaller cardinality result than selecting state alone. In 11g, it is possible to create extended statistics against two or more columns. The resulting metrics can be used by the optimizer to provide better access plans when both columns appear in a query.

```
BEGIN
  cg_name := dbms_stats.create_extended_stats
             (null,'customer_data',
             '(cust_state,cust_city)');
END;
/
```

```
SELECT sys.dbms_stats.show_extended_stats_name
        ('sh','customer_data',
        '(cust_state,cust_city)') col_group_name
FROM dual;
```

You will obtain an output similar to the following:

```
COL_GROUP_NAME
-----------------
SYS_STU#S#WF25Z#QAHIHE#MOFFMM
```

Expression Statistics

When a function is applied to a column in the where clause of a query (function(col1)=constant), the optimizer has no way of knowing how that function will affect the selectivity of the column. By gathering expression statistics on the expression function(col1), the optimizer will have a more accurate selectivity value. You can also use the **create_extended_statistics** function to accomplish this:

```
SELECT dbms_stats.create_extended_stats
                (null,'customer_data',
                '(lower(cust_city))')
FROM   dual;
```

Use Adaptive Cursor Sharing

Using bind variables in queries allows for the most effective use of server memory, as a single cursor can be created for a given SQL statement and then shared multiple times even as the values of the bind variables change. However, when bind variables are used against columns containing skewed data, the execution plan created for the original cursor can be less than optimal. This happens because the optimizer 'peeks' at the value of the bind variable(s) during the initial hard parse of the SQL statement. The values presented to the optimizer on the first statement are treated as representative of all subsequent values. In Oracle 11g, the concept of Adaptive Cursor Sharing has been implemented to resolve this issue. Adaptive Cursor Sharing allows the server to compare the effectiveness of execution plans between SQL statements with different bind variable values. If it detects suboptimal plans, it allows for the use of alternate execution plans for the same statement. This functionality is always enabled and neither requires nor allows any configuration. There are two concepts regarding Adaptive Cursor Sharing that you must be aware of.

- **Bind-Sensitive** -- Cursors where the optimizer has determined the optimal execution plan is dependent on the bind values are tagged as bind-sensitive.
- **Bind-Aware** -- Bind-sensitive cursors for which the optimizer has created alternate execution plans dependant on the bind values are tagged as Bind-Aware.

Diagnose performance issues using ASH

Oracle's active session history (ASH) samples the current state of all active sessions. The data is collected into memory where it can be accessed via the V$ACTIVE_SESSION_HISTORY view. AWR snapshot processing also writes the information to persistent storage. Active sessions are sampled every second and the results stored in a circular buffer in the SGA. Active sessions are any connection that is waiting for an event that does not belong to the Idle wait class.

Capturing only active sessions allows Oracle to keep the data to a manageable size. The ASH data allows administrators to analysis current data using the V$ACTIVE_SESSION_HISTORY view and historical data by using the DBA_HIST_ACTIVE_SESS_HISTORY view. The data also contains execution plan information for each captured SQL statement. ASH data can be rolled up on various dimensions, including:

- SQL identifier of SQL statement
- SQL plan identifier and hash value of the SQL plan used to execute the SQL statement
- SQL execution plan information
- Object number, file number, and block number
- Wait event identifier and parameters
- Session identifier and session serial number
- Module and action name
- Client identifier of the session
- Service hash identifier
- Consumer group identifier

Oracle can create Active Session History reports that are useful for diagnosing transient performance problems. These problems may not appear in the Automatic Database Diagnostics Monitor (ADDM) analysis. ASH reports are created in an HTML format and are divided into multiple sections. Oracle recommends using Oracle Enterprise Manager to generate ASH reports. However, it is also possible to generate ASH reports via the ashrpt.sql script, located in the ORACLE_HOME/rdbms/admin directory.

The contents of the ASH report are divided into the following sections:

- **Top Events** -- The top wait events of the sampled session activity categorized by user, background, and priority.
- **Load Profile** -- The load analyzed in the sampled session activity.
- **Top SQL** -- The top SQL statements of the sampled session activity.
- **Top PL/SQL** -- Lists the PL/SQL procedures that accounted for the highest percentages of sampled session activity.
- **Top Java** -- Lists the top Java programs in the sampled session activity.
- **Top Sessions** -- Describes the sessions that were waiting for a particular wait event.
- **Top Objects/Files/Latches** -- Lists the database objects (such as tables and indexes), database files, and latches that accounted for the highest percentages of sampled session activity.
- **Activity Over Time** -- Provides details about activities and workload profiles during the analysis period.

ABOUT THE AUTHOR

Matthew Morris is an Oracle Database Administrator and Developer currently employed as a Database Engineer with Computer Sciences Corporation. Matthew has worked with the Oracle database since 1996 when he worked in the RDBMS support team for Oracle Support Services. Employed with Oracle for over eleven years in support and development positions, Matthew was an early adopter of the Oracle Certified Professional program. He was one of the first one hundred Oracle Certified Database Administrators (version 7.3) and in the first hundred to become an Oracle Certified Forms Developer. In the years since, he has upgraded his Database Administrator certification for releases 8i, 9i, 10G and 11G, become an Oracle Advanced PL/SQL Developer Certified Professional and added the Expert certifications for Application Express, SQL, and SQL Tuning.

Made in the USA
Monee, IL
04 November 2026

67378121R00144